THE
vegucated
FAMILY TABLE

Irresistible Vegan Recipes & Proven Tips for
Feeding Plant-Powered Babies, Toddlers & Kids

♡ Marisa Miller Wolfson

Marisa Miller Wolfson
& Laura Delhauer

with Reed Mangels, PhD, RD

Photography by Erin Kunkel

TEN SPEED PRESS
California | New York

To my children
—Marisa

To my parents
—Laura

To the former kids
who dreamed of being
superheroes, and now have
kids of their own, who can
be. This book is for you.

—both of us

CONTENTS

FOREWORD
by Genesis Butler

Genesis Butler is an thirteen-year-old animal rights and environmental activist and TEDx speaker who received the Animal Hero Kids' Sir Paul McCartney Young Veg Advocate award, the Vegan Kid of the Year award from Vegans Are Cool, PETA's Youth Activist of the Year, and the Lisa Shapiro Youth Activist award.

I wasn't raised vegan from birth. When I was four, I asked my mom where chicken nuggets came from and when she told me, I became a vegetarian. When I was six, I saw my mom breastfeeding my younger sibling and asked where our milk we drink every day came from. Once I found out how it comes from cows, I became vegan. Basically, as soon as I found out how animal products were made, I didn't want anything to do with them.

When I went vegan, my parents and siblings started including vegan foods in their diets, and now my entire family is vegan. My mom was able to veganize a lot of our favorite traditional recipes—which was really important for us. For example, before we went vegan, we would always make tamales—and my mom thought that she'd never be able to eat them again. But we played with different vegan recipes and now we have our own delicious version—and everyone in my extended family loves it, too! That's why I'm excited about *The Vegucated Family Table*, so more families can see how easy it is to veganize recipes and enjoy the vegan lifestyle together.

I'm grateful that my parents are so supportive about my choices and my activism. My mom always travels with me for conferences and speaking engagements, and my dad stays home to

watch my three siblings. It's a big family effort—and sometimes we all go to protests together! But activism is nothing new for my family. My great-granduncle Cesar Chavez was a successful, plant-based labor organizer. Most importantly, he made sure farm workers were treated fairly, and he never gave up making the world a better place for other people because it really mattered to him. He did a lot of public speaking, and when I studied him I saw how much of an impact that had on masses of people. I've taken his example to heart in approaching my own activism, filled with hope and community.

My family isn't my only support system. I've made a lot of vegan friends who hold the same values, goals, and dreams as me. That's become very important to me because sometimes people don't understand how serious and urgent it is for people to adopt plant-based diets. It's nice to have friends to relate to on those issues.

My friends at school are often curious about vegan food and what I like to eat. I enjoy sharing meals with them and encouraging them to try vegan food, and they are usually receptive and excited to try new things! But if they're interested in adopting a plant-based lifestyle, they can have a hard time getting their parents' support. I do my best to provide them with food options, research on nutrition, and examples of how animals are treated so that they can discuss everything with their parents. Sometimes it feels like a lot of weight to carry, but I am grateful to my large vegan community for support. We need more family-friendly cookbooks to show how eating vegan is possible for anyone. I know that

The Vegucated Family Table is going to help facilitate conversations between parents and children, while providing delicious and nutritious recipes that everyone will love.

Being introduced to a plant-based lifestyle as you grow up is extremely important. If kids are fed meat, they often do not connect that it comes from an animal—and even if they ask about what they're eating, they receive answers like "chicken nuggets" or "a burger." Because of that, kids can become desensitized to the issue and not associate their food with the process it comes from. I think that people who are aware of veganism are inherently more conscious of the food they are eating and are more likely to grow up to be healthier and more compassionate.

With the climate crisis we are in, it is more important than ever to raise kids vegan and to take note of how animal agriculture affects the planet. Kids who are vegan can all become climate change activists because the issues are closely connected. As a young animal rights and environmental activist, I have always felt that it is our responsibility to do something to save our planet if we want to have a healthy Earth when we are adults.

I love how Marisa and Laura write about how vegan kids can feel like superheroes. Going vegan definitely made me feel like a superhero because I became aware of all of the ways the planet, animals, and your own health benefit. Recently, Marvel Universe contacted me about joining their Hero Project on Disney Plus, which features real life superheroes making change in the world. A superhero protects beings, cares about everyone, and can influence others to do good—and that is my goal as a vegan. I think everyone can be a superhero!

INTRODUCTION

If you've thought about transitioning your family to a more plant-based diet, or if you've decided to raise your child completely vegan, this book is for you.

If you've read in baby food books how it's "really hard" to raise a baby on such a "restricted" diet and that you should "talk to your doctor" (who likely had less than a day of nutrition education in all her or his years in medical school), this book is for you.

If you're tired of feeling like a crappy parent because you fed your toddler chicken nuggets ("to get some protein") made with a white starch for the umpteenth time this week since he doesn't like to eat colors and *he has to eat something, dammit*, this book is for you.

If your little one rejects meat or has an egg allergy or a dairy sensitivity and you've heard that vegans have some weird and witchy formula for getting their kids the nutrients they need without these things, please enter our coven, for our secrets are wondrous and abundant, and this book is for you.

If you've ever been told that feeding your kids a vegetarian or vegan diet will make them social outcasts and they'll end up in the school dumpster, this book is for you.

If you really love animals and you really love the planet and oh my God you love your baby so much but you want to make sure you're giving her the best and healthiest start in life, we wrote this book for you.

We're glad you're here, and hey, let's get crazy in the kitchen, because parents need some way to maintain a sense of adventure. But first we'll tell you a little bit about who we are so you have a sense of what we're about, what we're doing here, and why we're doing it.

Marisa:

When I decided to forgo animal products eighteen years ago, raising *children* without milk, meat, dairy, eggs, and fish was the last thing on my mind. I was a greenie and an animal advocate, after all, and I wasn't sure I even wanted to burden the planet with kids. Fast-forward ten years, and there I was, suddenly visible in the public eye because I had made a vegan documentary, *Vegucated*, and because I was very pregnant. Well-meaning family members who knew I was a staunch vegan had the balls (the *balls*!) to send me warnings about raising my child on a plant-based diet . . . as if I hadn't already done my homework, as if I didn't already know what nutrients to be mindful of, as if I didn't have a growing network of vegan parent friends whose kids were winning track meets, excelling in school, and proud as hell of being vegan.

When I was pregnant, I fantasized about having a healthy son who would still look rosy in spite of his wardrobe of cream-colored natural, organic clothes, who ate steamed kale, and who petted pigs at farm animal sanctuaries with me. I felt heady from the power and joy of it all—the idea that I could set the foundation for a lifetime of loving the foods that do the best job of preventing disease and ensuring my son a long, happy life . . . Gah! It's what every health-conscious crunchy mama dreams of.

But then Gabriel came along, and he made it clear that he was not there to fill my crunchy mama fantasies. He was a real person with his own likes (processed vegan cheese!) and dislikes (steamed kale!), and I had to let go of a lot of control. I also scrambled to find resources to give me ideas for how to expand his palate and get him to love as many healthy plant-based foods as possible. At the time, there were no cookbooks aimed at parents of vegan babies, toddlers, or young kids. I relied mostly on inspiration from other vegan parents, in real life and online. We discovered new favorites and new ways to incorporate kale (see Perfect First Green Juice, page 124), and Gabriel, now age seven and a proud animal-loving vegan, is thriving. So is his sister, who, by the way, really likes kale, especially in chip form (see Baked Kale Chips, page 131).

Meanwhile, I would constantly get emails from other plant-powered parents with health or food questions and requests for recipe ideas and inspiration. It seemed that they, too, needed the book I had searched for in vain. And then brrrring! (magical chime sound)—the idea for this book was born. I was pumped and ready to write.

Then something unexpected happened: I became preggo again and got back into baby-planning mode. Shortly before my daughter, Emmeline, was born, I hired a vegan mother's helper, knowing how hard it is to juggle a toddler and a newborn when your husband works long hours and travels often. This helper was the lovely Laura Delhauer, an actor/theater producer/childcare provider. I discovered that she was also a naturally gifted cook, so I took the burp cloth and the baby and handed her the apron. She even helped get Gabriel to eat more veggies. From her work as a nanny, she had experience getting kids who had been raised on the standard American toddler diet of chicken nuggets and buttered noodles to love foods like green peas and hemp seeds. We turned my home kitchen into a test kitchen and reached out to plant-powered parent friends for their mainstay recipe contributions, and we haven't looked back.

Laura:

I'm a writer and performer, and about nine years ago, I accidentally stumbled upon an additional art form in plant-based cooking. It started as a hobby because a loved one was having some health issues. I'm a solution-oriented person and an empath. Seeing people I love (or strangers, for that matter) in pain of any kind is something I've never handled well. I needed solutions. I initially only learned about the health benefits of cutting out animal-based foods. But as I continued down this road and watched my loved ones getting healthier just as I was getting healthier, I suddenly needed to learn all that I could about the benefits of plant-based living.

I read every book I could find, watched documentaries, attended events, and took classes, and I was shocked to discover not only the nutritional benefits, but the massive environmental benefits of consuming more plants and fewer animals. And eventually, albeit reluctantly, I did a deep dive into how meat is processed and how animals and humans are treated so that we can eat meat every day. I wanted no part in that. And being solution-oriented, I got cooking.

I didn't go to any fancy culinary school, though I've enjoyed taking classes at the Natural Gourmet Institute. I learned to cook in my tiny studio apartment with my boyfriend between rehearsing Chekhov scenes for acting class. I learned to cook by deciding with a friend that it would be fun to teach plant-based cooking out of our tiny Brooklyn kitchens. I learned to cook with absolutely no structure or technique but all kinds of curiosity and love—the only way to do anything, in my opinion.

Then one day, Marisa walked into my life and offered to pay me to be the messy, unstructured, technique-free cook that I was.

I have worked with children in theatre, as a swim coach, and as a nanny, and my wish for all the incredible kids I've known is that they never struggle with that "why is my body failing me?" mystery, whether it be a body image issue or an illness. We now have the information to empower our children and set them up for a less stressful, more disease-proof life, while contributing to a kinder, healthier planet. How cool is that? I'm glad to be participating in the conversation about the most progressive way to fuel this world's wonderful tiny humans.

Marisa and Laura:

The majority of our recipes center around whole foods and are meant for everyday meals, but we also have recipes that may be more indulgent or flexible for special occasions—birthdays, holidays, and when you just need to wow people. There are also ideas for when you really don't have time to cook—because we're real people and so are you, and ain't nobody livin' solely on Instagram-worthy plates of superfoods bathed in natural light.

We're delighted to have nutritionist and nutrition professor Reed Mangels on board to help answer nutrition questions and to highlight notable nutrients in our recipes to remind us that plant-based dishes are nutritional powerhouses. Reed is the foremost expert in the US on vegetarian nutrition for kids, and we're honored to have her expertise.

Finally, we want to take a moment to congratulate you on your general awesomeness. By picking up this book, by thinking hard about raising a kid with plant-based foods at the center of their plate, not the side, you are embarking on something huge and important. Every time you cook, every time you choose plant-based foods, you are ensuring a healthier planet for your kids. You really are engaging in environmental activism: you're saving water, saving land, reducing greenhouse gas emissions, and reducing water pollution. You're setting your child up for a lifetime of healthier eating habits, and that family favorite you discover now will likely become their comfort food later. What a gift: healthy comfort food! But what makes our hearts really sing is the connection that kids feel with their food when they live in a family that intentionally consumes plant-based foods. This diet—this way of thinking and seeing the world—taps into children's natural love of animals and of nature, and their fascination with what their bodies can do.

The days of growing up ignorant about the negative impacts of our consumption habits are behind us. People are aware now that the rain forest is ablaze to clear land for cattle grazing and growing cattle feed, the oceans are dying from overfishing, animal agriculture is a major contributor to greenhouse gas emissions, and the vast majority of farmed animals are mistreated. It's jarring to discover that the dairy industry takes calves away from their mothers just a few days or even hours after birth so her milk can go to humans. And male chicken hatchlings—even in the organic, free-range egg industry—are suffocated or ground alive because unlike female chicks, they don't grow large enough or fast enough to be sold for meat. When we were young, we didn't know. It wasn't our parents' fault—they didn't know, either. But kids today are likely to grow up hearing about these things, and that's good. This information needs to spread. Ignorance is not bliss. Knowledge is power. But by raising our children plant-based, we're allowing them to feel proud to be part of the solution rather than guilty about contributing to the problem.

What kid doesn't want to be a superhero? With this book, we can bring that fantasy to life. By eating plants, every kid can save lives and make the world a better place. And so can you. Let's get over the guilt and instead feel empowered and motivated to make change.

WHY PLANT-BASED?

The standard American diet (SAD) is pretty, well, sad. Sure, processed meats contain protein, but they also contain plenty of sodium, cholesterol, and, according to World Health Organization, the leading medical institution in the world, as many carcinogens as cigarettes. And cow's milk has calcium, right? Yes, it does, but so do a host of plant-based foods. Plant-based foods don't contain milk's addictive properties and growth hormones, designed by nature to keep calves drinking their mothers' milk so they can grow into great big cows. And what happened to those cows? How are any of these products processed? Most of us who grew up in the US were not encouraged to know where our food came from or how it got to our plate. Not knowing is no longer an option. Our choices are affecting the health of our families, other humans, the animals we share this planet with, and the planet itself.

We all want what's best for our children, so it seems we would want what's best for all children. But in the US, our demand for meat and dairy is so excessive that we are outsourcing the production of animals, and the grain and soy to feed them, to other countries to keep up with that demand. Meanwhile, the children in some of these countries are starving, and their indigenous communities are being displaced or even destroyed. The acceleration of climate change caused by animal agriculture and the disproportionate effect of those changes on low-income communities and communities of color is simply unfair. We're not horrible people for not knowing these things before now, but now that we know, we can act differently.

Feeding our families more plants is the clear choice—it's the only choice if we're going to send the next generations into a future with clean water to drink and clean air to breathe.

So let's cook some plants and make a difference!

VEGUCATED KITCHEN TOOLS

Whether you've been vegan for years or this is completely new territory, prepping your kitchen to fuel a whole plant-powered fam can feel daunting. But worry not! This section is here to vegucate you and set you up for success. First of all, no, you do not have to buy every fancy appliance, and no, you do not have to implement all these changes at once. Take your time getting vegucated and setting up your kitchen in a way that feels good for you and your family. To help you do that, let's talk kitchen tools, pantry essentials, and meal prep.

Class Requirements

These tools are required for at least one recipe in this book, but don't freak out and feel like you have to buy everything on the list. Implement things as they make sense for you and your fam.

Blender
A good high-speed blender is essential for a plant-based kitchen. We are big fans of the Vitamix, but we realize this is a large investment. A Vitamix can make sauces, spreads, purees, flours, and much more in seconds, which can be a godsend for parents, but any good high-speed blender will do.

Cooking spatula
This tool is essential for flipping pancakes and useful for your favorite sautés and tofu scramble.

Cutting board

Most any will do, but we would not recommend glass. A wood or bamboo cutting board will get much love in a plant-based kitchen.

Food processor

This is very helpful for making things like nut butter spreads and fast chopped nuts and veggies. If you have a Vitamix, you can use it to accomplish many of the same things that a food processor can. However, for a few recipes like our Energy Bites (page 138), Snacky Snakes (page 139), Chocolate-Hazelnut Spread (page 199), and Clean-Out-the-Fridge Burgers (page 179) we recommend a food processor.

Knives

A few good sharp knives can make food prep much faster, easier, and safer. We recommend having at least one sharp chef's knife, one serrated knife (for breads, tomatoes, etc.), and one paring knife (for small fruits and vegetables).

Rubber spatulas

Flexible spatulas (preferably one large and one small) are great for scraping batter out of mixing bowls, food processors, and blenders.

Baking sheets

Large skillet

Measuring cups

Measuring spoons

Mixing bowls

Muffin tin

One big pot

Parchment paper and/or silicone baking mats

Small saucepan

Steamer basket

Strainer

Wooden spoons

Whisk

Teacher's Pet

You can absolutely operate without these, but they can really enhance a vegucated kitchen.

Hand mixer or standing mixer

If you're Laura, a fork works just fine—not for frosting, though. For frosting/icing, one of these is kind of essential.

Juicer

The two juice recipes in this book (pages 123 and 124) are intended to be made using a juicer, but we recognize that this is an investment not everyone is interested in making, and that is A-OK. Juicing with your kiddos can be a fun way to get lots of nutrients in, but so can blending, so this is not essential.

Cast-iron skillet

Fine-mesh sieve

Grater

Wire rack

Extra Credit

These extra appliances can make life easier.

Air fryer

We were surprised to find that lots of parents have begun adding this luxury item to their kitchen. Definitely extra credit, but an air fryer can make healthier versions of yummy fried foods using a fraction of the oil of a deep-fryer. This appliance can also be used to deliciously crisp up certain baked foods.

Citrus juicer

An electric citrus juicer is the best way to get all the juice from your citrus fruits and do so very quickly. Not a necessity, but certainly helpful, and one of Laura's favorite appliances.

Instant Pot/slow cooker/pressure cooker

These can make easy batches of beans, soups, stews, and grains. A pressure cooker specifically can be a game-changer if you're dealing with lectin sensitivities or sensitive digestive systems.

THE VEGUCATED PANTRY

Let's have a serious talk about palm oil. Palm oil is currently found in almost half of all packaged products sold in US grocery stores. It has become the most widely used vegetable oil on Earth. But just because it comes from a plant does not mean its production is kind to animals, humans, or the planet. Palm oil is kind to none of these.

Most of the world's palm oil comes from the rain forests of Indonesia and Malaysia. In order to grow oil palms, corporations clear rain forests, displacing native species and indigenous peoples, often forcefully. These companies have also been found to use abusive labor practices, including child labor. Alongside the beef, dairy, oil, and natural gas industries, the palm oil industry is one of the leading causes of deforestation, which is greatly contributing to species extinction and climate change. This is clearly not something we want to participate in, right? But like we said, nearly half of all packaged products in your grocery store, from snack foods to shampoo, contain palm oil.

We have worked hard to keep the recipes in this book free of unsustainable palm oil. We also highly recommend reading labels before purchasing products, as well as downloading the Sustainable Palm Oil Shopping app.

You can learn more about this issue and become part of the solution by familiarizing yourself and your family with incredible organizations like Rainforest Action Network.

Making your family's meals and treats from ingredients you know and trust is a great way to be conscious consumers, so let's take a look at some of our pantry essentials.

Our Pantry Staples

Canned beans
Because they can make meal prep quick, we always keep a few different kinds of canned beans in the pantry. Chickpeas (garbanzo beans), black beans, baked beans, pinto beans, navy beans, adzuki beans, kidney beans—stock up! We do soak dried beans for our White Bean Wonder Waffles (page 112) and Clean-Out-the-Fridge Burgers (page 179), but we also know that busy parents don't always have the time or head space for that.

Coconut aminos
This is one of our favorite additions to savory recipes. Often used as a substitute for soy sauce, coconut aminos are about 70 percent less salty with a touch of sweetness as well. (No, it does not taste like coconut.)

Cooking oils and butter substitutes
If possible, it is best to use organic, minimally processed oils, and high-quality cooking oils can be part of a healthy plant-based diet. Our go-to oils are grapeseed, sunflower, and safflower oil for cooking, coconut oil for baking, and extra-virgin olive oil for dressings, sauces, and spreads. For a buttery spread and baking butter, we use Earth Balance or Miyoko's. If you prefer to avoid oils, replace them with vegetable broth or water in savory dishes. In baked goods, you can often substitute applesauce or mashed ripe banana for oil, but results may vary.

Egg replacements
Flax meal and chia seeds are both high in fiber and protein and great for digestion, and both can be turned into easy egg substitutes in baked recipes. Simply stir together 1 tablespoon chia seeds or flax meal and 3 tablespoons water and refrigerate until the mixture gels or develops a raw-egg-like consistency, 5 to 10 minutes.

Nutritional yeast ("nooch")
Generally understood to be a vegan's best friend and a vegan parent's absolute savior, this delicious, naturally cheesy-tasting powder is high in protein and essential B vitamins, and many brands include B_{12}. Nooch isn't like the

yeast you'd use for leavening bread. It's part of the fungi family and grows on molasses, then is washed and dried into a flaky powder. Nooch naturally contains iron, but some brands are fortified with even more. Not only is nooch included in many of our recipes to add cheesy flavor, but it's also excellent sprinkled on pretty much all savory foods, vegetables, greens, and—if you ask Marisa's daughter—bananas.

Sweet stuff

Our favorite sweeteners are coconut sugar (aka coconut palm sugar—from the coconut palm, which is completely unrelated to the plants used for palm oil), pure maple syrup, and Medjool dates. Healthier than their refined white sugar counterparts, they are pricier and not always as accessible. In all recipes calling for coconut sugar, you can use brown sugar or a granulated sweetener of your choice. Maple syrup and other liquid sweeteners, such as agave or coconut nectar, can be substituted 1:1. Medjool dates are heartier and softer than other dates, but if they are not available, you can use other dates in their place. If you are using them for baking, soak them in hot water to cover for a good 20 to 30 minutes first, then drain them; this softens them and makes them easier to work with. Just remember to remove the pits!

Vegetable broth

A good vegetable broth is essential for lots of savory soups and dishes. We love Better Than Bouillon Organic Vegetable Base, a paste that you whisk into water to make your veggie broth. One small jar makes nearly 10 quarts of flavorful veggie broth! (Pro tip: We use just slightly more than 1 teaspoon of the paste per cup of water to make extra-flavorful broth.) Better Than Bouillon makes many vegan broth bases, but please note that not all their products are vegan, so be sure to read the label carefully before purchasing.

TIPS FOR MEAL PREP

Leisurely evenings of meal preparation are not realistic in most homes on the daily. That being said, dedicating one day (or part of one day) each week to some serious meal prep can give you a whole week of less-stressful mealtimes.

If you're lucky enough to live near a farmers' market, perhaps you could plan your meal prep day on the day of your local farmers' market and let the in-season foods inspire the recipes you make for the week. However you shop, dedicating some time to meal prep can be a game-changer. Here are some things we love to make ahead.

Big Batches

Making a big batch of soup or stew, some lentils or beans, and some grains at the start of the week means endless possibilities for quick and easy meals all week long.

A batch of muffins (pages 133 and 134), Thumbprint Breakfast Cookies (page 111), Fudgy Nut-Free Energy Bites (page 138), and/or pops (see the Sips and Slurps chapter, page 119) can ensure yummy healthy breakfasts and snacks on busy days.

Purees

Purees are great freezer foods. Not only does a freezer stash of purees make it easier to feed your baby, but having some on hand means you can boost any smoothie, sauce, or soup with extra nutrition.

Sauces, Spreads, and "Sprinkles"

In our Sneaky Sauces, Spreads, and Sprinkles chapter (page 185), we have everything from chia jam and chocolate-hazelnut spread to cashew chive spread and peanutty dipping sauce to perfect quick pasta sauces. We love keeping jars of our "sprinkles" readily available to add fun, flavor, and nutrients to anything in a pinch.

ASK THE NUTRITIONIST

This chapter contains some of the most important information in the book. It is the chapter you can bookmark, send, or quote from to prove to skeptical friends and family members (Hi, Katie's dad! Hi, Derek's cousin who likes to forward articles!) that it's not only possible to raise your child vegan, but that with just a little bit of research and planning, doing so can have real advantages for your kiddo and can lead to excellent lifelong eating habits.

Lucky for Katie and Derek, we have Dr. Reed Mangels on board. Dr. Mangels, a reputable registered dietitian, has published articles on vegetarian babies and toddlers, looked at all the science on plant-based diets for babies and children and run it past the country's largest organization of nutrition professionals—and even written a position paper on vegan diets for all life cycles for that organization! Reed Mangels cowrote two position papers on vegetarian diets for the Academy of Nutrition and Dietetics (formerly the American Dietetic Association) after sifting through all the solid peer-reviewed research on the topic. She has a PhD in nutrition and taught in the nutrition department at the University of Massachusetts Amherst, she's been the Vegetarian Resource Group's nutrition advisor for the past thirty years, and she's a mom. She is also the author of *The Everything Vegan Pregnancy Book*, the go-to book for pregnant vegan mamas. This was Marisa's bible when she was pregnant with her two children, and many mothers know and trust Dr. Mangels as an authority on the topic. Here Dr. Mangels answers some of the most common nutrition questions that people have when it comes to raising vegan children.

Q: Everyone in my family worries that my baby won't have adequate nutrition if I raise him vegan. How can I reassure them?

A: It's easy to feel uncomfortable when family members question your child-raising decisions. Your best defense is figuring out the root of their concern and what they are really asking.

For example, are they concerned about health after reading about a vegan baby who had health problems? You can address their concerns by letting them know that these stories are usually case reports, meaning they are isolated incidents. Most vegan babies grow up to be healthy vegan children and adults. If you examine case reports, you'll see that these parents were excessively limiting the foods they fed their babies. It's simply not okay to give a baby only apple juice or to replace breast milk with a watery gruel made from oats or rice. Reassure your family members that you're planning to give your child a variety of healthy plant foods, including fruits, vegetables, whole grains, and legumes.

What if they have specific concerns like protein or calcium or iron? Luckily, you have a resource like this book. Its nutrition information will help you show the ways that you will meet your child's array of nutritional needs. You may also find it helpful to refer family members to the Academy of Nutrition and Dietetics's position paper on vegetarian diets, which states, "These diets [vegetarian, including vegan] are appropriate for all stages of the life cycle, including pregnancy, lactation, infancy, childhood, adolescence." If you've been fortunate enough to find a vegan-friendly pediatrician, talking about the doctor's positive take on vegan diets might help convince your family that such a diet can be nutritionally adequate.

Perhaps what your family members are really asking is, "Will I be able to make food that this child will be able to eat?" In this case, no matter how convincing you are about nutrition, questions will continue to come up, so you will need to answer the question that's not being asked, and perhaps continue to answer it for years to come. Talk to your family members about your plans for family dinners and other occasions. If it seems helpful, provide some simple recipes using easy-to-locate ingredients, and share hints for veganizing favorite meals. Offering to help family members prepare menus can go a long way toward achieving their acceptance.

And remember, families are concerned because they care. If they weren't questioning your child's vegan diet, they might be questioning your ideas for getting your baby to fall asleep or your other parenting practices.

Q: What are some of the health benefits specific to a vegan diet for babies and children?

A: Unfortunately, there's been almost no research on vegan babies and children to date. Lacking that, we can look to studies of vegetarian children. In these, we find that vegetarian children tend to eat more fruits and vegetables than their nonvegetarian peers. The same is likely true for vegan children. More fruits and vegetables means more of the good stuff: vitamin C, beta-carotene and other antioxidants, and phytochemicals. Vegan children's diets are typically lower in saturated fat and cholesterol than the diets of nonvegan children. Vegan children are not exposed to veterinary antibiotics found in foods derived from animals. And vegan children are likely to be familiar with a greater variety of whole plant foods than are nonvegan children. Greater familiarity often means greater acceptance. In other words, vegan children may be acquiring lifelong healthier eating habits.

One study found that nonvegan children with obesity who were placed on a no-added-fat vegan diet for four weeks experienced a decrease in blood pressure, weight, and blood cholesterol levels. Additionally, studies show that adult vegans have lower risks for high blood pressure, heart disease, and type 2 diabetes. Therefore, if a vegan baby or child goes on to be a lifelong vegan, she or he is likely to have a lower risk of several chronic diseases.

Q: The USDA revises its guidelines frequently—some of us grew up with the food pyramid, others with MyPyramid, and now there's MyPlate. What is your take on these guidelines? What does an ideal vegan meal plate for a kid look like to you?

A: The specifics of the USDA nutrition guidelines are revised approximately every five years as newer information becomes available. However, while there may be variations in the exact amount of saturated fat that is problematic or whether children should drink juice, the basics of a healthy diet remain. Guidelines always call for eating a variety of vegetables, fruits, and whole grains. Legumes (beans and peas) are often suggested as either a vegetable choice or a source of protein. These plant foods are the basis for a healthy vegan diet, one that includes plenty of vegetables, fruits, whole grains, and legumes.

The Dietary Guidelines for Americans, which are developed by the USDA and the US Department of Health and Human Services, have become increasingly friendly to vegetarians. In the 2015–2020 Dietary Guidelines, a vegetarian diet was named as one of three healthy eating patterns recommended for Americans. This healthy vegetarian eating pattern does include dairy and eggs, but, as the Dietary Guidelines state, "This pattern can be vegan if all dairy choices are comprised of fortified soy beverages (soy milk) or other plant-based dairy substitutes."

An ideal vegan meal plan for a kid would provide a variety of whole plant foods and enough calories to support growth, and would include:

Legumes, nuts, seeds, and nut and seed butters

Whole grains

Vegetables

Fruits

Fats and oils or foods supplying fats (like avocados and nuts)

Reliable sources of calcium, vitamin D, vitamin B_{12}, and omega-3 fats

Fortified soy milk or fortified pea protein milk is an easy way to supply protein, calories, vitamin B_{12}, vitamin D, and calcium. It's helpful to include a couple of cups a day in a meal plan for younger vegan children (ages one to three years) who are no longer breastfeeding or drinking a soy-based infant formula. Amounts of foods will vary depending on the child's age, weight, gender, and activity level.

Q: I know that there are plant-based sources of protein. Are they adequate? What is the recommended protein intake for babies, toddlers, and older children, and can my vegan kids get enough?

A: Plant-based sources of protein can supply adequate amounts of protein and essential amino acids (the building blocks of protein) for vegans of all ages. A myth that you may hear is that plant proteins are lacking one or more of the essential amino acids, the components of protein that must be supplied by food because they are not produced by the human body. While some plant proteins do have lower amounts of one or more essential amino acids compared to animal proteins, the amount of the amino acids in question is not zero, it's just less than what you'd find in cow's milk, for instance. Amounts of other essential amino acids may be higher than or similar to the amounts in animal-based protein.

By eating a variety of whole plant foods over the entire day, higher amounts of some amino acids in some foods will balance out the lower amounts of amino acids in other foods. Your vegan kids can get enough protein and essential amino acids.

Protein needs are based on your baby's or child's weight. Because protein in plant foods may be somewhat more challenging to absorb, nutrition professionals suggest that vegan children (and vegan babies, once they begin eating solids) get a bit more protein than the recommended dietary allowance (RDA). This slight increase in protein has been accounted for in the following recommendations:

7 to 12 months: 0.6 grams of protein per pound of body weight

1 to 3 years: 0.6 grams of protein per pound of body weight

4 to 13 years: 0.5 grams of protein per pound of body weight

So, if your two-year-old vegan toddler weighs 28 pounds, his or her protein needs would be 28 x 0.6—about 17 grams of protein per day. If you consider that a cup of soy milk or pea protein–based milk provides about 7 grams of protein, it's clear how easy it can be to meet protein needs if your child eats whole plant foods and includes legumes, whole grains, nuts, seeds, nut and seed butters, and vegetables.

Ten Good Sources of Protein for Vegans

1. Tempeh, ½ cup = 17 grams
2. Soybeans, ½ cup cooked = 15.5 grams
3. Veggie burger, 1 patty = 15 grams (this amount will vary by recipe or brand)
4. Tofu, extra-firm, 4 ounces = 12 grams
5. Lentils, ½ cup cooked = 9 grams
6. Peanut butter, 2 tablespoons = 8 grams
7. Black beans, kidney beans, chickpeas, lima beans, pinto beans, ½ cup cooked = 7.5 grams

8. Seitan, 1 ounce = 7 grams
9. Soy milk or pea protein–based milk, 8 ounces = 3 to 11 grams (most are in the range of 7 to 8 grams)
10. Almond butter, 2 tablespoons = 7 grams

Q: I'm having major trouble breastfeeding, and my supply is tanking. Is there a vegan formula that I can use for supplementing?

A: Technically speaking, there are no commercial infant formulas in the United States that are labeled as "vegan." Soy-based formulas are dairy-free but contain vitamin D derived from lanolin from sheep's wool. Some vegan families will opt to use a soy-based formula, recognizing that it is the safest available alternative to breast milk and that it is close to being vegan.

If you need to supplement breast milk or breastfeeding is not an option for any reason, commercial soy-based formula is the only safe alternative for a baby.

A board-certified lactation consultant can be invaluable to families having difficulties with breastfeeding. The International Lactation Consultant Association has a directory of certified consultants.

Some families have luck with donor milk, either from a lactating friend or a donor milk bank. There's no guarantee that the milk donor from a bank is vegan. In fact, it's highly unlikely. However, donor milk could be a solution for families who are comfortable with this option.

Q: I'm thinking beyond the boob. When should I wean my baby, and what milk should I give him when I do?

A: Weaning usually begins when your little one is about six months old. Up until then, the only thing they need is human milk, the perfect food for babies. At about six months, they're showing signs of being ready for solid foods. They should be able to sit up without a lot of support and to hold their head upright. They should no longer push food out of their mouth with their tongue but should be able to use their tongue to move food to the back of their mouth to swallow. They're likely to be interested in food, often trying to grab food from your plate or attentively watching you eat.

Starting them on solid foods doesn't mean the end of breastfeeding, however. The American Academy of Pediatrics recommends continuing to breastfeed for at least the first year after birth or longer as mutually desired by mother and infant. The World Health Organization calls for continued breastfeeding along with appropriate complementary foods up to two years of age or beyond.

Whether you choose to breastfeed for one year, two years, or longer, it's important to have breast milk be your baby's primary beverage for at least the first year. Of course, if you can't breastfeed for this long or your healthcare provider recommends supplemental feeding, a commercial soy-based formula is what you'll use. Soy milk, rice milk, other plant milks, and homemade formulas should not be used to replace breast milk or commercial infant formula during the child's first year.

After your baby's first birthday, if you (or your baby) are no longer interested in breastfeeding, it's time to think about what milk to give him as a primary beverage. If your child is growing well and eating a variety of foods, he can be transitioned to a fortified soy milk or pea protein–based milk containing calcium, vitamin B_{12}, and vitamin D. Low-fat or nonfat soy milks should not be used before age two. Ideally, the soy or pea protein milk would be unsweetened. It may be helpful to mix it with breast milk or the formula the child is familiar with at first, then gradually decreasing the amount of breast milk or formula in the mix. Milks based on rice, oats, hemp, almonds or other nuts, and coconut are not recommended as a primary beverage for infants and toddlers, as they are quite low in protein and calories. This book includes a recipe for Boosted Almond Milk (page 120), which Marisa used when her one-year-old son couldn't tolerate soy. If you decide to use this boosted milk in place of fortified soy milk or fortified pea protein–based milk, be sure to make it with an almond milk that is fortified with calcium, vitamin D, and vitamin B_{12}. Be aware that almond milk is low in some essential amino acids. If you're using this milk as your child's primary beverage, be sure that your child eats a variety of other protein sources, including legumes, whole grains, and vegetables, every day.

If there are any concerns about your child's growth or if she eats only a limited number of foods, hold off on introducing plant milks for a while and continue with breastfeeding or a commercial soy-based formula. Ask your healthcare provider or a registered dietitian nutritionist if you're not sure whether it's time to make the switch.

Q: How much calcium will my baby need as she grows? What are the best vegan sources of calcium?

A: Calcium is needed to support the growth of bones and teeth. For the first six months after birth, your baby gets all the calcium she needs from breast milk or a commercial infant formula. It's likely that breast milk or formula is also going to supply most of your baby's calcium up until age one. Good vegan sources of calcium like pureed kale, collards, or broccoli can be introduced before age one, but it's unlikely that the small portions infants eat will provide much calcium.

From ages one to three, the RDA for calcium is 700 milligrams per day. From ages four to eight, the RDA is 1,000 milligrams per day. It's completely feasible to get these amounts of calcium from vegan foods. One easy source is a calcium-fortified plant milk, ideally soy or

pea protein–based. These milks typically supply 300 to 450 milligrams of calcium in an 8-ounce glass. A couple of glasses of calcium-fortified plant milk will put you well on your way to meeting your child's calcium needs. Green leafy vegetables like kale, collards, turnip greens, and bok choy are also good sources of easy-to-absorb calcium, providing 75 to 100 milligrams in ½ cup of cooked vegetable. You may be surprised to learn that spinach isn't as good a source of calcium as you thought: It contains oxalic acid, which blocks the absorption of most of its calcium. However, spinach is rich in iron and other nutrients. Some children eagerly eat a plate of lightly steamed greens. If that's not your child, try blending greens into pasta sauce and making green smoothies. If you are concerned that your child is not getting enough calcium, consider a children's calcium supplement that does not exceed the RDA for calcium.

Ten Good Sources of Calcium for Vegans

1. Calcium-fortified plant milks, 8 ounces = 100 to 500 milligrams (most are in the range of 300 to 450 milligrams)
2. Calcium-set tofu (look for "calcium sulfate" in the ingredients list), 4 ounces = 200 to 400 milligrams
3. Soy yogurt with added calcium, 6 ounces = 300 milligrams
4. Calcium-fortified orange juice, 4 ounces = 175 milligrams
5. Collard greens, ½ cup cooked = 134 milligrams
6. Tofu processed with nigari (magnesium chloride), 4 ounces = 130 milligrams
7. Tahini, 2 tablespoons = 128 milligrams
8. Almond butter, 2 tablespoons = 111 milligrams
9. Turnip greens, ½ cup cooked = 98 milligrams
10. Tempeh, ½ cup = 92 milligrams

Q: What about iron supplements? Our pediatrician told me that the current recommendations for iron supplementation have been strengthened for breastfed babies, and she wants me to give our baby drops of an iron supplement every day. Is this a good idea, or is it overkill? What kind of supplement should I give? What are the best sources of iron in a vegan diet?

A: If your baby was born full-term and is healthy, it's likely that she has enough iron stored up to meet her needs for the first four to six months of her life. That's good, because breast milk is not especially high in iron. In order to reduce the risk of iron deficiency, pediatricians recommend that breastfed infants start taking a daily iron supplement at four months and continue the supplement until solid foods containing iron are introduced. The amount of iron recommended is 1 milligram for every kilogram your baby weighs (about 0.45 milligrams for every pound). Giving your breastfed baby iron drops is not overkill, because iron deficiency can negatively affect development.

One of the first solid foods many vegan families introduce is an iron-fortified baby cereal. This cereal can be mixed with expressed breast milk to make a soupy gruel at first. Fortified baby cereals are one source of iron. Other good iron sources for vegan babies and children include dried beans and peas; spinach; tofu; wheat germ; dried fruit (apricots, prunes, raisins); and whole grain or fortified breads, cereals, and pasta. See above right for a list of good sources of iron. Including a source of vitamin C in meals that contain iron will allow your baby's body to absorb more of the iron. For example, serve beans with tomato sauce, slice some strawberries to go along with iron-fortified cold cereal, and sauté tofu with broccoli.

Iron deficiency is a common issue for many young children, whether they're vegans or not, because children often don't eat enough iron-rich foods. If, despite encouraging your child to eat lentils and hummus, raisins, and spinach, your child's iron is low, a low-dose iron supplement or a multivitamin with iron can help. Unless advised otherwise by a physician, choose an iron supplement that does not exceed the RDA for iron: 7 milligrams per day for one-to-three-year-olds and 10 milligrams per day for four-to-eight-year-olds.

Ten Good Sources of Iron for Vegans

1. Tofu, ½ cup = 6.6 milligrams
2. Lentils, ½ cup cooked = 3.3 milligrams
3. Spinach, ½ cup cooked = 3.2 milligrams
4. Tahini, 2 tablespoons = 2.7 milligrams
5. Kidney beans, ½ cup cooked = 2.6 milligrams
6. Chickpeas, ½ cup cooked = 2.4 milligrams
7. Soybeans, lima beans, black-eyed peas, ½ cup cooked = 2.2 milligrams
8. Tempeh, ½ cup = 2.2 milligrams
9. Swiss chard, ½ cup cooked = 2 milligrams
10. Cashews, ¼ cup = 2 milligrams

Q: I hear zinc is a nutrient for vegans to be mindful of, and that it's important for immune function. How can we up our zinc consumption?

A: Zinc is important for immune function but it's also known to support normal growth and development. Zinc is also needed for the proper functioning of our senses of taste and smell.

Zinc is found in many whole plant foods, often along with substances called phytates that reduce the amount of zinc the body absorbs. So, it's important not only to up zinc consumption but also to take steps to make sure more of that zinc is absorbed. The RDA for zinc is 3 milligrams per day for one-to-three-year-olds and 5 milligrams per day for four-to-eight-year-olds.

So, how do we increase zinc consumption? Eat more whole plant foods that supply zinc, including beans and peas; tofu and other soy foods; quinoa, millet, barley, and brown rice; nuts and nut butters; seeds and seed butters; and fortified foods including breakfast cereals, energy bars, and some veggie "meats."

Ten Good Sources of Zinc for Vegans

1. Peanuts, ¼ cup = 2.3 milligrams
2. Pumpkin or squash seeds, hulled, ¼ cup roasted = 2.2 milligrams
3. Tofu, firm, ½ cup = 2 milligrams
4. Adzuki beans, ½ cup cooked = 2 milligrams
5. Cashews, ¼ cup = 1.9 milligrams
6. Sunflower seeds, ¼ cup = 1.8 milligrams
7. Sunflower seed butter or cashew butter, 2 tablespoons = 1.6 milligrams
8. White beans, ½ cup cooked = 1.5 milligrams
9. Tahini, 2 tablespoons = 1.4 milligrams
10. Lentils, chickpeas, black-eyed peas, ½ cup cooked = 1.2 milligrams

And how can you make sure more zinc is absorbed? Here are some ideas. Choose yeast-leavened or whole-grain sourdough baked goods over products leavened with baking powder, since they allow the body to better absorb zinc. Zinc is also better absorbed from sprouted beans and grains. Eating foods that supply zinc along with foods containing citric acid or other organic acids increases zinc absorption somewhat. For instance, eating soy or coconut yogurt, sauerkraut, or citrus fruits or juices along with a plant source of zinc makes the zinc more available.

And if you're concerned about your child getting enough zinc, check to see if her multivitamin/mineral supplement supplies zinc.

Q: I hear there's a difference between the omega-3s from fish versus omega-3s from plant sources. What is the difference, and what's the best source?

A: To put it simply, there are small differences in the chemical structure of EPA and DHA, the omega-3 fatty acids from fish, and that of ALA, the omega-3 from plants. ALA is an essential fatty acid, meaning that we need to get it from foods because our bodies can't make it. We can make some EPA and DHA from ALA, but only a very small amount of ALA is converted to EPA, and even less to DHA.

Good sources of ALA include flaxseed and flaxseed oil, canola oil, and soy products. Exclusively breastfed infants whose mothers are well-nourished will get the ALA they need from breast milk. ALA is added to commercial infant formulas.

As infants begin eating solid foods, small amounts of flaxseed (about ¼ teaspoon of ground seeds per day) can be used to supply additional ALA. Infants can also get ALA from small amounts of canola oil, flaxseed oil, hemp seed oil, walnut oil, and other foods including wheat germ and chia seeds. See page 18 for ten good sources of ALA for vegans. The Adequate Intake (intakes of or above this amount are unlikely to be inadequate) for ALA is 700 milligrams for children aged one to three years and 900 milligrams for children aged four to eight years.

DHA is thought to play a role in the development of the brain and the retina. Vegan DHA is made from microalgae, which is where fish get their DHA. Breastfeeding vegans are often encouraged to take 200 to 300 milligrams per day of vegan DHA supplement to increase the amount of DHA in their breast milk. DHA is commonly added to commercial infant formulas.

Experts don't know for certain if vegan children need DHA supplements. No studies using DHA supplements have been done with vegan children or children who don't eat fish or seafood as subjects. In both of these situations the children's diets do not supply DHA. Vegan parents may opt to give their children a vegan DHA supplement of 100 milligrams per day.

Ten Good Sources of ALA for Vegans

1. Flaxseed oil, 1 teaspoon = 2,420 milligrams
2. Tofu, firm, ½ cup = 733 milligrams
3. Chia seeds, 1 teaspoon = 713 milligrams
4. Flaxseed, ground, 1 teaspoon = 570 milligrams
5. English walnuts, 3 halves = 515 milligrams
6. Soybeans, ½ cup cooked = 500 milligrams
7. Canola oil, 1 teaspoon = 433 milligrams
8. Soybean oil, nonhydrogenated, 1 teaspoon = 311 milligrams
9. Hemp seeds, hulled, 1 teaspoon = 289 milligrams
10. Tempeh, ½ cup = 206 milligrams

Q: How can we prevent vitamin D deficiency? Are vegans any more prone to deficiency?

A: Vitamin D's main function is to promote the absorption of calcium. Bone health suffers when babies and children don't get enough vitamin D. Vitamin D is only naturally found in a limited number of foods. It is added to some brands of plant milks and yogurts. In addition to getting vitamin D from foods, our bodies can make vitamin D following sunlight exposure.

It's challenging to get enough vitamin D from foods, whether you're a vegan or a nonvegetarian. Vitamin D–fortified plant milks typically have 100 to 140 IU of vitamin D in an 8-ounce (1-cup) serving. Children aged one year or older need 600 IU of vitamin D. Do the math: That's 4 to 6 cups of fortified plant milk a day, much more than most children drink. Other vitamin D sources supply even less, and many foods that are fortified with vitamin D, like orange juice and breakfast cereals, use a nonvegan form of the vitamin.

And then there's sun. Most pediatricians recommend limiting sun exposure for infants and young children because of the risk of skin cancer later in life. Limited sun exposure, sunscreen usage, dark skin, clothing, winter, and pollution all keep our skin from making the substance that goes on to become vitamin D.

From limited vitamin D in food sources to the dangers of frequent sun exposure and many other factors, vitamin D supplements are recommended for vegans and nonvegans alike to prevent deficiency.

Exclusively breastfed infants and partially breastfed infants getting less than 32 ounces (4 cups) of infant formula per day should be given a daily supplement of 10 micrograms (400 IU) of vitamin D. This recommendation is for all infants, vegan or not, because breast milk contains only small amounts of vitamin D.

After weaning, a vitamin D supplement for children should not exceed the RDA of 15 micrograms (600 IU) per day. If your child is taking a multivitamin/mineral supplement, check to see if it supplies this amount of vitamin D. If it does, or if it supplies less and your child's vitamin D–fortified plant milk makes up the difference, additional supplementation is not needed.

Two different forms of vitamin D are used in supplements and fortified foods. Vitamin D_2 is vegan, and is also called ergocalciferol. Vitamin D_3, also called cholecalciferol, is typically not vegan. However, a plant-sourced vitamin D_3 has been discovered and is being used in vegan supplements. You can check the label to see which type of vitamin D a supplement contains. Both forms of vitamin D can effectively prevent vitamin D deficiency.

Good Sources of Vitamin D for Vegans

1. Vitamin D–fortified plant milks, 8 ounces = 80 to 240 IU
2. Vitamin D–fortified vegan yogurt, 6 ounces = 60 to 80 IU

Q: Do I need to be concerned about vitamin B_{12}? How much does my child need? What foods provide it?

A: Vitamin B_{12} is an essential nutrient for everyone because of its role in developing and maintaining brain and nervous system function. It's especially vital in pregnancy, lactation, infancy, and early childhood because of its importance to brain development. Vegans need to be aware of good sources of vitamin B_{12}. Plant foods do not contain significant amounts of vitamin B_{12}, so vegans need to look to B_{12}-fortified foods or supplements to get this vitamin in their diets.

The amount of vitamin B_{12} a child needs depends on the child's age. Exclusively breast-fed infants whose mothers are using reliable sources of vitamin B_{12} every day do not need an additional vitamin B_{12} source. The same is true for infants exclusively fed a commercial infant formula or a combination of infant formula and breast milk from a woman who is conscientious about meeting her vitamin B_{12} needs.

Once they begin eating solid foods, vegan infants and children need to get vitamin B_{12} from either supplements or fortified foods. The RDA for vitamin B_{12} is 0.5 micrograms per day from six to twelve months, 0.9 micrograms from one to three years, and 1.2 micrograms from four to eight years.

Vegan foods that are commonly fortified with vitamin B_{12} include some brands of plant milks, some veggie meats, some energy bars, some tofu, some nutritional yeast, and various other foods. You can see a list of good sources of vitamin B_{12} for vegans at right. Be careful: Not all products are fortified, and product formulations can change. If a particular food is the main source of vitamin B_{12} for your child, check the Nutrition Facts label frequently to ensure the formulation continues to meet your child's needs. Try for a couple of servings a day of foods fortified with vitamin B_{12}.

Most children's multivitamins supply vitamin B_{12} and are a simple way to meet your child's vitamin B_{12} needs. Look for a multivitamin that supplies at least the RDA for vitamin B_{12}. There's no real advantage to taking a large dose of

vitamin B_{12}. If your child doesn't use a multivitamin supplement or if her multivitamin doesn't contain vitamin B_{12}, and if your child doesn't eat enough fortified foods every day to meet the RDA, look for an age-appropriate vitamin B_{12} supplement. Supplements that contain at least 10 micrograms of vitamin B_{12} (5 micrograms for age six months to one year) can be taken once daily.

Good Sources of Vitamin B_{12} for Vegans

1. Red Star VSF nutritional yeast flakes, 1 tablespoon = 4 micrograms

2. Vitamin B_{12}—fortified plant milks, 8 ounces = 0.6 to 3.6 micrograms

3. Vitamin B_{12}—fortified tofu, 3 ounces = 1.2 micrograms

- Serve your child a variety of whole plant foods. For example, offer all different colors of vegetables—green, orange, red, purple, white, and so on—over a week or two. Different vegetables and fruits have different vitamins and minerals, so a variety helps cover all the nutritional bases.

- Encourage your child to eat legumes, whole grains, fruits, and vegetables every day. While it may be tempting to some children to only focus on bread and pasta, add some beans and vegetables and offer fruit and nut butters for snacks. That's a way to promote variety.

- Processed foods like store-bought veggie burgers and plant-based yogurt can be used to add variety, but should be used occasionally, at most. These foods can have a lot of added salt or sugar, and may not be especially nutritious. Use whole plant foods (like those in the recipes in this book) most of the time.

- Remember that toddlers have small stomachs and get full quickly. Offer regular healthy snacks between meals. If you or your child's healthcare provider are concerned about the child's growth being on the low side, you may need to offer more concentrated calorie sources in place of some of the bulky low-calorie foods often eaten on a plant-based diet. For example, offer avocado cubes instead of (or along with) carrot sticks. Sauté vegetables in a little oil instead of serving them raw in a salad.

- Use supplements and/or fortified foods to make up for shortfalls. Vegan parents especially need to make sure their children are getting enough iron, zinc, calcium, vitamin D, and vitamin B_{12}.

- A food guide can be helpful as you start thinking about how you're going to feed your child. The nutritional guide on page 22 is a starting place. It is based on six food groups plus an additional milk group for one-to-three-year-olds. Your children may need more food depending on their age and activity level.

4. Vitamin B_{12}—fortified veggie burger, 1 patty = 0.9 micrograms

5. Vitamin B_{12}—fortified vegan deli slices, 3 slices = 0.9 micrograms

6. Vitamin B_{12}—fortified vegan energy bar, 1 bar = 0.6 micrograms

Q: Now I'm daunted by these nutritional recommendations. Do I need to count out grams of each nutrient?

A: It can be overwhelming to think of all the different nutritional recommendations! There are a few general guidelines to keep in mind to make it likely that your children are getting what they need nutritionally.

There will be days when they don't precisely eat according to the guide, and that's okay. For the most part, however, this guide is one way to meet the majority of your children's nutritional needs. Fortified foods or supplements will be needed to supply an adequate amount of vitamin D and vitamin B_{12}.

- Fortified soy milk or pea protein–based milk is an easy way for one-to-three-year-olds to get the protein, calcium, vitamin D, and vitamin B_{12} they need once they're no longer drinking breast milk or infant formula. These milks can be served by the glass as well as be used in cooking. Smoothies or ice pops (like Purple Porridge Breakfast Pops, page 114; Neverland Smoothie, page 122; and Pink Drink, page 122) are other ways to serve plant milks. Choose unsweetened versions of plant milks. Other plant milks—including almond milk, rice milk, oat milk, and coconut milk—don't provide much protein and are often low in calories. They can't replace soy milk or pea protein–based milk for children.

- A variety of legumes, nuts, seeds, and nut and seed butters provide protein, iron, zinc, and other nutrients. A four-year-old's servings from this group could include scrambled tofu for breakfast, hummus dip (with crackers, vegetable sticks, and fruit slices) for lunch, a smoothie made with a pea protein–based milk for a snack, and lentil-tomato sauce on pasta for dinner.

- The grain products group offers so many choices. Think of the variety of bread eaten worldwide and of grains including barley, corn grits, rice, quinoa, and farro. If a child's diet is already very high in fiber, it's okay to serve him some refined grains; they can provide calories without excess bulk.

- When thinking about this food guide, don't feel as if your three-year-old child has to eat one huge serving of vegetables every day. Vegetable servings can be spread over several meals and snacks. For instance, a three-year-old might have 2 tablespoons of cooked carrots for lunch, ¼ cup of red pepper strips for a snack, and ¼ cup of stir-fry made with a combination of snow peas, broccoli, and mushrooms for dinner.

- Whole fruits can be overwhelming for small children. Try cutting apples and oranges into smaller pieces just before serving.

- Children need fat in their diets. Toddlers don't need to be on a low-fat diet; they need the calories that fats provide. Also, fats promote the absorption of some vitamins. The oils, seeds, and nuts listed in the Comments column of the food guide are good sources of ALA, an essential fat (see page 22).

- Some foods are especially good sources of calcium, and these are listed in their own group. They can be counted in more than one food group; for example, ½ cup of cooked broccoli would be counted as both a serving of vegetables and ½ serving of calcium-rich foods.

Q: Should I give my child a multivitamin? If so, which kind and when do I start?

A: Although there's no requirement for children to take a multivitamin/mineral supplement, many parents find that a child-friendly supplement provides some peace of mind, especially on those days when it seems as if a child has decided to live on air.

Vegan children can meet their needs for most nutrients by eating a variety of whole plant foods. It's just that not every child eats a variety of foods every day. If your child is especially picky, using a multivitamin/mineral supplement makes it more likely that her needs for important vitamins and minerals are being met. Of course, supplements don't supply protein or calories and don't take the place of a healthy diet.

When choosing a supplement for your child, look for one that is age-appropriate, that is vegan, and that provides both vitamins and

NUTRITIONAL GUIDE
FOR VEGAN CHILDREN

Food Group	Serving Size	Number of Daily Servings for a 1-to-3-Year-Old	Number of Daily Servings for a 4-to-8-Year-Old	Comments
Milk	1 cup fortified soy milk or fortified pea protein–based milk, or soy-based infant formula or breast milk	2	See right	Milks are included in the legumes, nuts, and seeds group for 4-to-8-year-olds. Milks should be fortified with calcium, vitamin D, and vitamin B_{12}.
Legumes, nuts, and seeds	½ cup cooked legumes or tofu or tempeh; 2 tablespoons nut or seed butter; ¼ cup nuts or seeds; 1 ounce meat analog; 1 cup fortified soy milk or pea protein–based milk	1 to 1.5 (in addition to 2 servings of fortified soy milk or pea protein–based milk)	4 or more	
Grain products	1 slice bread; ½ cup cooked rice, pasta, or other grain; 1 ounce breakfast cereal	3 or more	6 or more	Grain products should be mainly whole grains.
Vegetables	½ cup cooked; 1 cup raw	1 or more	4 or more	
Fruits	1 medium fruit; ½ cup cooked or canned fruit	2 or 3	2 to 4	
Fats and oils	1 teaspoon oil or vegan butter spread	2 or 3	2 or more	Use ¼ teaspoon flaxseed oil, or 1 teaspoon canola oil, or 1 teaspoon ground flaxseed, or 3 English walnuts halves once (for 1-to-3-year-olds) or twice (for 4-to-8-year-olds) daily.
Calcium-rich foods	½ cup calcium-set tofu or calcium-fortified plant milk; ¼ cup almonds; 2 tablespoons almond butter or tahini; 1 cup cooked broccoli, kale, collard greens, or mustard greens	See the milk group above for primary sources of calcium	6 or more	These foods can count both as servings of calcium-rich foods and as servings from other food groups.

This food guide provides minimum amounts. Children may need additional food to provide adequate calories.

minerals in amounts that do not exceed the RDAs for your child's age. A good multivitamin/mineral supplement will include vitamins A, D, and E; thiamine; riboflavin; niacin; vitamin B_6; vitamin B_{12}; folic acid; pantothenic acid; biotin; calcium; iron; zinc; magnesium; iodine; selenium; copper; manganese; and chromium.

Usually multivitamin/mineral supplements are not used in the first year because the littlest ones' nutritional needs are met, for the most part, by breast milk or commercial infant formula. They're also not often needed in the second year because most toddlers are eating a variety of foods and still may be breastfeeding or drinking infant formula. The story may change around age two or three. At that point, because their growth rate slows and because there are so many exciting things to do besides eating, children may be less interested in food. If that's the case, a multivitamin/mineral supplement can help to meet their needs. A registered dietitian nutritionist can help to assess your child's diet and determine if a supplement is needed.

For information about supplements of iron, vitamin B_{12}, vitamin D, and DHA, see the FAQs for each of these nutrients.

Q: My child seems to be smaller than her peers, but the doctor isn't worried since she's on her growth curve. Am I being paranoid?

A: In the US, children's growth is evaluated using growth charts from the World Health Organization (for babies and children from birth to two years old) and from the Centers for Disease Control and Prevention (for children aged two years and older). These growth charts feature a series of percentile curves that provide an idea of what normal changes in weight and height or length look like. For example, if your child's length is at the 25th percentile, that means that 75 percent of children of your child's age are longer and 25 percent are shorter than your child. These differences in length are often due to genetic factors.

A wide range of growth percentiles are considered "normal." A baby or young child can be between the 2nd and 98th percentiles for weight and length or height (5th to 95th percentile for age two and older) and still be considered within the healthy range. If your child is in this range, even though she's smaller than her peers, it's likely that her growth is okay. Physicians use growth charts along with other measurements to assess a child's growth, which may also explain her doctor's lack of concern. One possible explanation for your child being shorter than her peers is that her parents are shorter. If she was born prematurely, she's also likely to be shorter than her peers.

Children usually stay near the same percentile for weight and height or length, so the fact that your child is doing this is reassuring. If a child's growth pattern changes, further assessment is needed. One important question is whether her measurements were done accurately. They may need to be repeated; if the repeat measurements confirm the original measurements, the child may need to come in for more frequent measurements or additional assessment.

Q: My daughter ate such a variety of foods as a baby, but now as a toddler, she's getting really picky. Should I be concerned?

A: It can be frustrating to have your child go from enthusiastically eating everything from avocados to zucchini to refusing anything except peanut butter, pasta, and apples. There are some common reasons toddlers become more particular about what they eat.

First of all, eating is something they can control. They've learned the power of "no" and practice using what seems to be their favorite word all the time. They're also becoming more aware of the world and realizing that it can be a scary place. Neophobia, the fear of new or unfamiliar things, is not uncommon in toddlers, and the new thing could be a person or a food. Food jags, where a child eats one or only a few foods almost exclusively, may be due to a toddler's needs for rituals. Rituals, such as eating the same foods, provide a sense of security and of control.

Toddlers are entering a period where they're not growing as quickly as they did when they were babies. Remember, babies triple their birth weight and increase in length by 50 percent in their first year. Imagine how big they would be if they kept up this rate of growth! This slower growth means they're just not as hungry, and they're often too busy exploring their world to want to spend a lot of time eating.

Unlike adults, toddlers probably won't eat some of everything on the table. They may eat a particular food with great enthusiasm one day and turn it down the next. They are also likely to eat great quantities of food at one meal and virtually nothing at the next. They tire of even their favorite foods. Yet studies show that over time, toddlers tend to eat a variety of foods and achieve a nutritionally adequate diet.

If a toddler is growing normally (see page 23 for more about this), it's likely that she's getting enough calories. Ideally, though, she'd be eating some grains, some beans, and some fruits and vegetables, even if the variety is limited. Check in with your child's doctor if your child's growth is concerning you or if she eats an extremely limited diet day in and day out.

There are strategies for working with toddlers. One thing to keep in mind is that it can take ten to fifteen (or more) exposures to a food before it becomes familiar. And "exposure" may not mean that the toddler eats the food. They may touch it, smell it, lick it, or taste it gingerly. Over time, especially if these experiments don't get a lot of attention, the food is likely to become part of their repertoire. And even though it's tempting to remind them that they didn't like the food before, it's probably best to not mention it.

Parents, caregivers, siblings, and friends are important role models for toddlers. Model healthy eating behaviors, and your toddler may give that broccoli a try.

Parents and caregivers are responsible for offering age-appropriate foods that meet the child's nutrient needs and for providing meals and snacks that include both familiar foods and new ones. Parents are responsible for deciding when meals and snacks are offered, and timing them so that snacks don't interfere with the next meal. Toddlers should be the ones deciding how much they eat. Large portions can be intimidating. Try starting with a couple of tablespoons and encourage the child to ask for more if she is still hungry.

One day you'll realize that your child (or perhaps your teenager) is once again eating a variety of foods. Your quiet persistence definitely has paid off!

Q: Some people are really hatin' on soy these days, and others are piling on the praise. Is soy bad? Is there such a thing as too much soy and are some forms of soy better than others?

A: There's a lot to like about soy. Soy foods, like tofu, tempeh, and soy milk, are excellent sources of protein, and can supply iron and zinc. Soy foods fortified with calcium, vitamin D, vitamin B_{12}, and other nutrients can be important sources of these vitamins and minerals for vegan children. And there's some evidence that eating soy products early in life is associated with a reduced risk of breast cancer later.

Soy foods contain relatively high amounts of isoflavones, which are described as plant estrogens. Because of the presence of isoflavones, concerns have been raised about potential hormonal effects of soy. Although there are only a limited number of studies on children and soy, the evidence suggests that eating moderate amounts of soy does not have adverse effects on development.

What is a "moderate" amount of soy? There's no hard-and-fast rule. A couple of servings a day seems reasonable. Basing most meals on soy seems like too much soy. So, if your child is used to eating soy yogurt for breakfast, soy milk and pretzels for a snack, a tofu burger at lunch, and a stir-fry with tofu at dinner, think about replacing some of the soy with chickpeas or other beans, nut butters, or pea protein–based milk.

There's no evidence that some forms of soy are better than others. Using tofu and other less-processed soy foods more often than commercial tofu burgers and soy ice cream can allow you to control the amount of added salt and sugar in your child's food.

Q: How can I prevent food allergies? When should I introduce soy, wheat, and nuts?

A: One recommendation for reducing your child's risk of developing a food allergy is to exclusively breastfeed her for the first four to six months. After that, foods can be introduced gradually, with a few days of observation between introducing one new food and introducing the next, so you can see if any signs of food allergy or sensitivity develop. If you believe that your baby has diarrhea or a rash or has been vomiting and you think it is a reaction to a food she ate, talk with your baby's doctor about whether that food needs to be avoided.

Parents used to be told to wait a year or more to introduce foods that were more likely to cause allergic reactions. That's no longer the case. After six months, infants can be given baby-safe versions of foods that are or contain common allergens such as soy, wheat, and nuts. Of course, giving a baby or young child whole or large pieces of nuts would be a choking hazard. Nuts need to be finely ground, or in nut butter form, and added to other foods like cooked grains to ensure they do not cause choking.

Specific guidelines for the introduction of peanuts were released by the National Institute of Allergy and Infectious Diseases in 2017. These guidelines divide babies into three groups:

Babies who don't have any eczema or food allergy

Babies who have mild to moderate eczema

Babies who have severe eczema (need to be treated with prescription creams often) and/or an egg allergy

The first group of babies can have products containing peanuts at any point once they are eating solid foods. For this group, there's no reason to rush to introduce peanut products, but there's no reason to wait, either.

The second group of babies should try peanut products around age six months, after you discuss this with the baby's doctor. Before introducing the food containing peanuts, the infant should be introduced to other solid foods to make sure she is developmentally ready for solid foods.

The third group of babies should be tested for peanut allergy and the introduction of peanut products should be discussed with the baby's doctor. The first taste of peanut products may need to be given in the doctor's office.

Whole peanuts and chunky peanut butter are choking hazards. It's safer to give babies smooth peanut butter mixed into other foods, or snacks made with peanut butter.

SOCIAL STUFF, SCHOOL, AND CELEBRATIONS

Awareness and knowledge of veganism has shot up as much as the availability of vegan food products has. The number of kids with food allergies or sensitivities has skyrocketed, and conscious consumerism is on the rise as well. So it's no longer considered strange to bring special food to the cafeteria, parties, or playdates. Millions of parents around the world are already calling teachers and other parents ahead of time to find out what's being served at special occasions so they can plan accordingly.

Still, a concern some parents maintain about raising plant-powered kids is the social stuff: that a child will struggle socially because he or she is vegan. This is understandable, as wanting our kids to fit in is a common concern of all parents, vegan or not. Too often, though, we forget to think about the flip side of what raising a child plant-based can do for them socially: It opens your child up to an expanding community of conscious, compassionate individuals, which contributes to their deep sense of purpose and can lead to lifelong bonds rooted in similar values. In this chapter, we will address how to find community and how to handle social situations in which your child might be the only veg kid, and put your mind at ease that there are practical solutions and exciting opportunities for your child to grow his sense of self and share that with other children.

RAISING A CONFIDENT VEGAN

Every vegan kid we know today who is old enough to understand why they are vegan views this aspect of themselves with pride. What kid doesn't want to see themselves as special, as an animal rescuer, as a planet saver, powered by food that helps keep their body healthy, clean, and strong? So much of the success of navigating social situations is predicated on a child's own healthy self-image. We interviewed a few adults who were vegan since birth about how they were able to have the self-confidence to navigate being a little kid in a big nonvegan world with aplomb.

Carey Kidd grew up vegan in Raleigh, North Carolina. He said, "I constantly dealt with the uneducated on what it was to be vegan. 'Vegan' wasn't even a term many people knew about during the nineties." But, he said, "My family was always supportive with everything I chose to do. My parents both taught me about self-respect and confidence—that it doesn't matter what people say or do as long as you're doing right by your own word."

We asked vegan-since-birth Sarina Farb if she had any advice to give parents on raising confident vegans, and she said, "My advice is to make sure you talk to your kids about veganism and why you are vegan! They need to be knowledgeable and equipped with information to answer comments and questions from their peers. For small children, this might be as simple as 'We don't eat animals because animals are our friends' or 'Cow's milk is for baby cows.' It doesn't have to be complex, but children need to be able to take ownership of why they are vegan and feel proud about it when they go out into the world."

Anne Dinshah, who is also vegan since birth, suggests, "Educate and inform [your kids] of the consequences of the choices they can make. Introduce them to animals at sanctuaries, let them help buy groceries and make food, involve kids in planning delicious dinner parties for a variety of friends, especially thinking about what vegan dishes the nonvegan people would like to eat. Empower kids to make their own decisions. They will be deciding for themselves the first time they go to a friend's house or to school anyway. Don't get overly concerned if they elect to try something that's not vegan occasionally; maybe they were hungry, curious, or unsure what to do."

If the child feels secure in his lifestyle, he will take social challenges in stride. This is not to say he may not have his moments, and parents handle these difficulties differently. Some value clear boundaries and consistency while others let go of ideas of perfection in trying moments and let their child have the nonvegan item on some special occasions. And anyone with a tween or teen knows that even their most secure vegan child may buckle under social pressure or even rebel at times and sneak nonvegan food. It's all developmentally appropriate, and it may be a phase. What's important is that you have shared your values with your child and given them a unique perspective from which they can see the world.

Sarina calls being vegan "the biggest blessing" of her life. "I am incredibly grateful to have been raised vegan! It has shaped my life and passions today, and I can't begin to imagine not being vegan. One of the biggest things that being raised vegan taught me is how to think critically about everything and not just accept the mainstream narrative at face value. When you see past the propaganda from the meat and dairy industry that promotes animal-product consumption, you realize that other things we are being told by government, advertisers, and the media may not be exactly as they appear. Veganism taught me to think for myself, and look deeply into issues before deciding what to believe."

Sarina, who was raised in Kansas, credits her vegan community as a major source of support for her growing up. Even though Kansas is "not the first place you think of as a vegan heaven," says Sarina, she and her family did manage to find "a small group of other families that were a mix of vegetarian and vegan and would at least have vegan gatherings and potlucks together." But for her, Vegan Summerfest, an annual conference held in Pennsylvania, is where she found the greatest sense of community. "As a kid, it was the main place I got to hang out with other vegan kids, and also I didn't have to ask what the ingredients were in anything. Some of the kids that I met at Summerfest are, to this day, some of my biggest inspirations and best friends. The environment there is so supportive, inclusive, and normalizing of veganism that it allowed me to feel like I fit in somewhere special."

Summerfest played an even more vital role in many vegan kids' lives before veganism became more popular as a valid lifestyle choice. On a societal level, people have become increasingly more tolerant of others who do their own thing. Millennials, who are generally less afraid to be different, are more altruistic and tend to value tolerance and diversity, and they're transferring these values to their children. Still, it is healthy and important for kids to have a sense of community, and even if you can't commune with other vegan families at Vegan Summerfest, you can still find your peeps. Not only do online vegan parenting groups help parents find answers to questions, share tips and resources, and troubleshoot challenges, but social media platforms such as Facebook and Meetup.com help local vegan families find each other. Marisa's kids feel instant kinship with other vegan kids, so they make a point of organizing playdates with these families and organizing or attending special holiday events produced by the local veg family meetup group, from Fourth of July picnics to Halloween parties, which we will discuss more in this chapter.

But first . . . what to do when a vegucated kid goes to school?

VEGAN AT SCHOOL

Schools and teachers are responding to the growing vegetarian and vegan student populations in large and small ways. Some school systems are implementing Meatless Mondays, and more and more are incorporating daily vegetarian or vegan options. Organizations such as the Coalition for Healthy School Food empower parents and students with road maps for how to get vegan entrées and options into cafeterias.

Even if you can't get your child's school to change its menu, you can certainly help make the classroom and even school events vegan-friendly for your kid. Sarina said, "My parents were wonderful!" and described how they were "very instrumental in pushing the school to have more inclusive snacks available for the children in general, and made sure that whenever there was a birthday party at school, they always sent me with a special treat or got the teacher to provide a vegan option."

Being "forced" to bring in an attractive vegan alternative to nonvegan classroom treats can lead to a new passion for baking and decorating, as it has for Marisa. YouTube is full of tutorials, and a quick trip down the Pinterest rabbit hole can provide hours of distraction—er, inspiration.

Tips for working with your child's school

- Create an open line of communication with the teacher on celebrations where food will be served so you can bring a vegan option for your child or, if you have the time/resources/know-how, a vegan treat for the whole class.

- To save yourself time and headaches, see if there is a classroom freezer where you can stash a small batch of cupcakes (or other treat) that the teacher can pull from any time there is a celebration. Switch them out every month or so.

- Sometimes parent friends are excited to go the extra mile to be inclusive and offer to make the birthday cake or cupcake for their kid's class party vegan. You can make things easier by suggesting that they look for cake mixes and frostings made by Cherrybrook Kitchen, which are not only vegan, but also free of common allergens; their products are available at well-stocked supermarkets and health-food stores.

- If snacks are provided in school, contact the teacher before the first day and inquire about any known allergies in the classroom, then provide them with a list of vegan-friendly snacks that are safe for all the children to eat.

- If your child's classroom has cooking or baking projects, share tried-and-true classic recipes that kids tend to love (like Chocolate Chip Banana Muffins, page 133) with their teacher.

- Get involved in bake sales and offer to contribute vegan options.

- Get involved in any other fund-raiser where food is sold or served, and suggest vegan options or offer to bring some.

BIRTHDAY PARTIES

"Aren't you afraid your kids will be missing out on the variety of foods at birthday parties?" an interviewer asked Marisa for a local news piece on vegan parenting. What variety? This man clearly did not have children, or he'd know that 95 percent of all birthday parties in the US feature pizza and cake. So, let's talk about pizza and cake. Different vegan families handle this differently. Some bring their own homemade pizza, some are able to pick up a vegan pizza along the way (lucky ducks!), some keep a stash of store-bought vegan pizzas in their freezer, and some just pull the cheese off whatever pizza is being served at the party. At one party we recently attended at Chuck E. Cheese, the chef agreed to use Daiya vegan cheese we brought from home for our kids' pizza. Score! Now, as for the cake . . . well, it's Vegan Parenting 101 to know to bring your own cupcake, and the beauty is that you can customize it to whatever your kid likes—flavors, colors of frosting, sprinkles, and so on—so they don't feel like they're missing out. You may be surprised how often nonvegan kids at the party say, "Heeey, I want one of those!"

Every once in a blue moon, the main party food isn't pizza, so be sure to contact the birthday child's parents well in advance to find out what will be served, so you can bring a vegan version or alternative.

And what about food for your own child's birthday party? Even if you don't have a specifically vegan pizza place near you, some pizza places do have a vegan option or can come up with one if you give them enough warning. But there is a whole world out there beyond pizza. Bagels and vegan cream cheese are perfect for a party in the morning, and finger sandwiches are perfect for a party at lunchtime. Or you can get sneaky and schedule the party nowhere near a mealtime, and just offer snacks such as cut-up fruit, veggies or crackers with hummus, pretzels, and popcorn.

Let's get to the focal point of every birthday party spread: the cake. More and more local bakeries and cake vendors know how to make vegan cakes, but if that isn't an option, we've got you covered—this book has some delectable cake and frosting recipes. Have cake-focused reality TV shows inspired you to get fancy with fondant? Most mainstream store-bought fondants are accidentally vegan. Satin Ice and Wilton brand fondants can be found at local cake supply or craft supply shops. If you want a more rain forest–friendly, palm oil–free vegan fondant option (which we recommend), Fat Daddio's will hook you up with several colors; they are available online. Many food colorings and sprinkles are vegan, and more and more companies such as Supernatural and Color Garden are sprouting up that make them with all-natural ingredients. Websites such as SaraKidd.com and Veganbaking.net and Facebook groups like the Vegan Cakes & Cake Decorating group are great resources for tips on vegan cake baking and decorating.

HANDLING KID-CENTRIC HOLIDAYS

When people contemplate raising vegan kids, one of the first concerns is the holidays. Will Easter still feel like Easter without real eggs to dye? Will my kid spontaneously combust when she finds out she can't eat any of the mini Hershey's bars she gets in her trick-or-treat bag? After getting just a couple of holidays under their belts, parents soon realize they can veganize the food and keep all the fun. The beautiful thing about raising kids vegan from babies onward is that the vegan traditions are all the children know and will be what they love and remember fondly as adults. What a beautiful gift—to consciously start traditions that are more in alignment with your values and not just do them because "that's how it's always been done."

And if you're looking for a little company so your kid doesn't feel left out, get some vegan friends together! Hosting vegan events is a great opportunity to get vegan families together and to share vegan food with nonvegans as well.

Vegan parents have gotten super creative in veganizing their kid-centric holiday traditions, and local health food stores and online shops keep making it easier and easier to find vegan holiday sweets.

Valentine's Day

Here are Valentine's options that are cholesterol-free and healthier for your heart:

- Boxes of vegan chocolates that can be ordered online
- Chocolate-dipped strawberries: Melt vegan chocolate chips in the microwave or in the top of a double boiler, thin the melted chocolate with some canned coconut milk, and stir until smooth, then dip away!

- Chocolate truffles you can make with your kids (see Fran Costigan's book *Vegan Chocolate* for many, many drool-worthy chocolate recipes)
- Heart-shaped cookies (see our Shape Cookies for Any Occasion, page 216), decorated with Royal Icing (page 218) and/or sprinkles
- Heart-shaped pancakes/waffles/toast at breakfast or a heart-shaped sandwich at lunch
- Love-themed bath bomb
- Pink Drink (page 122)
- Valentine's Day–themed books

Easter

Easter is a weird holiday as it is: We celebrate the resurrection of Jesus Christ by searching for dyed chicken eggs left behind by a rabbit? Let's veganize this wackiness! How about compostable, plant-based-plastic Eco Eggs filled with:

- Bouncy balls
- Cereal
- Coins
- Figurines
- Gummy snacks
- Healthy snacks like grapes, blueberries, dried fruit, or sunflower seeds
- Mini pretzels
- Stickers
- Tattoos
- Vegan chocolate eggs or chocolate chips
- Vegan jelly beans

Kids love opening eggs and finding surprises inside. If you miss the painting/decorating aspect of Easter eggs, check out wooden Easter eggs that can be purchased online and painted. Or you can jump on the rock-painting bandwagon and paint rocks in bright Easter colors or with inspirational messages and then hide them around the neighborhood for others to discover.

No egg hunt is complete without Easter baskets. Here are a few ideas of what can go into an Easter basket beyond eggs and vegan jelly beans:

- Art supplies: paints, pencils, markers, chalk
- Bubbles
- Eco-Dough or Play-Doh
- Egg-shaped fossil dig kits
- Hatching toys
- Jump rope or balls
- Stuffed animals
- Toys and books
- Vegan chocolate bunnies or chocolate eggs found online

Halloween

Whether it's anxiety about dealing with sugar highs and cavities or worry that your kid will want to eat all the milk chocolate— or gelatin-filled goodies that her friends are eating or (holy goodness) that there's unsustainable palm oil in everything (see page 7), Halloween can feel spooky for newly vegan and eco-conscious parents. But we witchy veteran veg parents have all kinds of tricks.

First of all, so much Halloween candy is accidentally vegan anyway that there will be no shortage of sugary goodies. And to check which ones are free of unsustainable palm oil, download the Sustainable Palm Oil Shopping app (if you haven't already!). There are companies that make lower-sugar, organic, or natural candies as well. Before a sweets-driven holiday, Marisa pops over to veganessentials.com to see what their latest offerings are. Here is a sampling of some vegan candies that are Roundtable of Sustainable Palm Oil–approved.

Note: Many candies are potential choking hazards, so always exercise caution.

- Annie's Organic Bunny Fruit Snacks
- Bottle Caps
- Enjoy Life chocolate minis variety pack
- Jolly Rancher hard candies and lollipops
- Loving Earth chocolates
- Nerds and Now & Later
- No Whey! Choco No No's
- Skittles, Smarties, Stretch Island Fruit Co. fruit strips, and SweeTarts
- Twizzlers
- Wholesome Organic Bunny Lollipops, Organic DelishFish, Cinnamon Organic Bears
- YumEarth assorted lollipops, hard candies, sour twists, fruit snacks, licorice, and more
- ZotZ

You may be asking, what do you do with the candy that isn't vegan? First of all, an educated, outspoken kid can help maximize vegan candy and minimize nonvegan candy by asking which ones are vegan, turning it into a teachable moment for the candy giver. Marisa's kids do that, and they do end up with more vegan candy, as well as bemused smiles from candy givers. Once home, her kids sort out the nonvegan candy and put it back in a basket that goes on the front stoop for late trick-or-treaters to take in passing, or they set it aside for nonvegan friends.

There are many creative ways to handle nonvegan or otherwise unwanted candy. Sayward Rebhal, author of *Vegan Pregnancy Survival Guide* and Magic Beans contributing chef (see page 167), gets a little help from a helper. "Our son Waits has grown up with the Switch Witch! She's besties with the tooth fairy, and she visits the homes of vegan kids and kids with allergies on Halloween night. She switches out all the nonvegan/allergenic candy for vegan/safe versions (or toys, depending on the family)."

Many dentists throughout the country offer prizes for Halloween candy that's brought in. Rockin' Raw chef Tere Fox takes her kids to their dentist's office, where "they will trade the kids' candy for gold coins to use in their prize towers, which are those small toy dispensers you see in diners and some grocery stores. My kids love our tradition and never complain."

If you are feeling ambitious, you can also make your own healthier vegan treats to replace any nonvegan treats your kids bring home. Laura's homemade almond butter cups (see page 207) were developed out of her love for her favorite childhood Halloween candy.

One recipe contributor and *Vegan Fam in Cow Town* podcaster, Amy Bradley, changed a potentially alienating-for-vegan-kids trick-or-treating experience into one that fosters community. At their annual "trunk-or-treat" in Columbus, Ohio, many vegans get together in a parking lot and turn their decked-out vehicles into trick-or-treating stations. She says, "Each year we turn our van into a shark and watch the creativity of a vegan community come together for the kids with special food, prizes, music, and games."

Thanksgiving

While Thanksgiving isn't a super kid-focused holiday, there are ways to get kids involved, whether having them help choose and prepare dishes for the meal or help choose a farm animal at an animal sanctuary to sponsor. Vegan mama Reasa Currier says her family "placed our adopted animal's pic on the table during the holiday meal." That's certainly the most humane way to have a turkey at the Thanksgiving table . . . unless you're serving food to a turkey! This is exactly what happens at farm animal sanctuaries all over the country. They treat their rescued turkeys to a feast of squash, pumpkin pie, kale salad, and cranberries. The humans also enjoy a vegan feast and some sanctuary time with the animals.

Hanukkah

Vegans shred their knuckles on graters making vegan latkes just as much as nonvegans making nonvegan latkes do, and vegan latke recipes abound on the web as well as in vegan holiday cookbooks. *Mayim's Vegan Table* by vegan actor mama Mayim Bialik has a latke recipe as well as an easy rugelach recipe, which Marisa made with her daughter for her preschool class's vegan Hanukkah celebration. Sharing vegan Hanukkah food and recipes in classroom celebrations is a great way to celebrate Jewish culture and plant-based living. Thanks to clearly marked kosher labels, vegan chocolate Hanukkah gelt is pretty accessible—if not at local Jewish centers or stores, then online.

Christmas

So much of the joy (and the stress) around Christmas is about the hype leading up to the big day.

Marisa carries on her German mother's tradition of giving her children advent calendars. There are so many options to choose from, including calendars with pictures, vegan milk chocolate (thanks to companies like Moo Free and No Whey!), or Legos behind the doors.

Santa Claus will be glad to know that the vegan cookies left out for him contain zero cholesterol. Shape Cookies for Any Occasion (page 216) are perfect for icing and decorating.

But Santa isn't the only one who requires cookies at this time of year. Our little elves work diligently in the kitchen each December for one of our favorite Christmas traditions: the vegan holiday cookie swap hosted by our friends Annie and Michael Walsh and their daughters. Annie attests, "Our vegan holiday cookie swap allows families to get together in a fun, festive way and enjoy a variety of holiday treats to take home, so that you only bake one batch but get lots to enjoy throughout the Christmas/New Year season."

LUNCHY SCHOOL MUNCHES

More and more schools are incorporating vegan entrées into cafeterias, but if your child isn't in one of those or is a touch picky, you will have many packed school lunches in your future. We write more about how to handle the issue of being vegan at school on page 29, but here we hope to inspire parents with some packed lunch ideas and share some sustainable options for some of the equipment you might need.

Packed lunches sure have changed since we were kids. Peanuts and tree nuts have been banned from many cafeterias and day cares, and sugary drinks are now nutritional no-nos. Not to mention the single-use plastic baggies whose molecules are still hanging out in our soil and water decades later.

Eco-minded parents have more options now than ever. ECOlunchbox and PlanetBox make stainless-steel lunch boxes, with separate compartments for various components of the meal. Planetbox ones have decorative magnets so your kid can personalize hers, and if your daughter is over her "space" phase and is now crazy about soccer, you can simply swap out the magnets instead of trashing the whole lunch box.

Amy Bradley alternates between reusable silicone bags and recycled paper baggies for her son's sunflower seed butter sandwiches. In her podcast, she also tells how she stocked up on miscellaneous silverware at a local thrift store to use for school lunches. In case that fork doesn't return home, it's not a big loss and won't leave a gap in her silverware set.

Now for the more challenging part: how to fill the lunch box with nutritious foods, safe for any-one with allergies, and quick to pack during a morning rush, that your kid will actually eat and will keep him full and happy for the rest of the day . . . or at least until snacktime.

We hope the lists on page 37 will help with lunch inspo. Some of these ideas are updated, veganized takes on lunch box classics, and some overlap with our snacks and sweets chapters, but most are based off the main meals and sides found in this book that might be leftovers from what you cooked last night . . . or even leftovers from last night's take-out. But it's handy to see our ideas in list form so you can mix and match from various categories.

If you belong to the camp of parents who look with envy, slight disdain, and more than a smidge of distrust at social media photos of perfect lunches teeming with greens and fruits cut into special shapes, then you are our people. Nevertheless, here are some ideas for making lunches and less-prized veggies or fruits a little more exciting for your children . . . including cut-ting fruits and veggies into cute shapes. Ha.

A search on Etsy for "mini cookie cutter" will bring up a lot of adorable options. Kiwis, bananas, cucumbers, large carrots, bell peppers, large strawberries, sandwiches, and waffles are all good candidates for cookie cutouts. Just be sure to put a dish towel or an oven mitt between the palm of your hand and the cookie cutter before you push down on it.

Another way to tell your little angel that you're thinking of her is to write a little note or draw a little picture on the peel of her banana.

Putting together a healthy, well-rounded lunch doesn't require a nutrition degree. Just try to make sure you have some fruit, some veg, and some protein in there. School lunch may not be the time to experiment with new foods, since that could be all your kid will get to eat for six hours or more, but some parents do find that their children actually eat better at school due to a little positive peer pressure from friends or teachers.

SAMPLE BALANCED PEANUT-FREE LUNCHES

Classic Vegan Kid Lunch

Sunnybutter Sammie (page 164)

Roasted Herbed Chickpeas (page 143)

Baked Kale Chips (page 131)

Kiwi and strawberries

Iron Sink Cookie (page 214)

Easy Breezy Lunch

Hummus wrap

Carrots

Apple slices with Caramel Sauce (page 200),
Medley of raisins and sunflower seeds

I Just Really Like Breakfast Lunch

White Bean Wonder Waffles (page 112),
cut into strips, with maple syrup to dip

Sweet Potato Wedges (page 94), with
ketchup to dip

Melon chunks

My Moms Like to DIY Everything Lunch

Tofu Dill Bites (page 173)

Broccoli Heart and Carrot Sticks (page 130)
with Cashew Chive Spread (page 196) if nuts
are allowed, or with hummus, if they're not

Banana with a nice message written on it

Fudgy Nut-Free Energy Bites (page 138)

My Parents Got Take-Out Last Night Lunch

Avocado sushi rolls

Edamame

Cucumber

Clementine segments

Simple Stuffed Date Halves (page 140)
made with sunflower seed butter

Their Alarm Didn't Go Off This Morning Lunch

Magic Beans (page 167)

Seaweed snack sheets, like those from SeaSnax

Dried mango

Soy yogurt and blueberries

Annie's Chocolate Chip Bunny Grahams

WHEN DINNER WON'T MAKE ITSELF AND LORD KNOWS YOU DON'T HAVE TIME TO COOK

The trick about raising kids is that they have to eat every day at least three times a day. It's all very tiresome, especially when you're in less-than-ideal situations (on vacation/at Grandma's house/during a busy weeknight) and have a picky eater or someone who is having a hypoglycemic fit over something unimportant.

People assume that if you are raising plant-powered kids, you spend hours in the kitchen every day chopping, steaming, marinating, and sautéing. You certainly can, but some days it's just not in the cards, even for the most devoted-to-healthy-cooking parent. In those cases, you can make a meal that's "assembled" rather than cooked, or else cooked with quick convenience foods that you enhance or pair with healthier items for a more nutritious meal.

Here are tips that may prevent the low-blood-sugar blues and get a meal on the table, STAT!

The Freezer Is Your Friend

Baby, toddler, and little-kid portions are pretty darn small, so what seems like a small amount of a dish can go a long way. Whenever we make soups, stews, pasta sauce, or casseroles, we spoon out some extra portions into small airtight containers and toss them in the freezer. (It helps to label the containers with the date and contents.) We also individually wrap muffins or veggie burger patties in aluminum foil or toss extra waffles in a freezer bag. It's easy to reheat any of these when you don't have time to cook.

Breakfast or Lunch for Dinner

Most toddlers can't tell the difference between breakfast, lunch, and dinner. Use this to your advantage. Peruse Lunchy School Munches (page 35) for ideas for "assembling" balanced meals.

Quick-and-Easy Cooking with a Little Store-Bought Help

Packaged convenience foods are high in sodium and/or processed, not to mention pricey, but they do serve a purpose when you need something that's, well, convenient.

- Pasta with a quick peanut sauce (peanut butter mixed in a blender with water, scallions or onion powder, and tamari). Serve with raw carrot and cucumber and store-bought baked tofu cubes.

- Microwave-baked potatoes topped with canned vegetarian baked beans and/or vegan butter and nutritional yeast.

- Canned beans with diced tomatoes or jarred salsa, thawed frozen corn, avocado chunks, and store-bought vegan sour cream.

- Amy's nondairy burritos, topped with vegan sour cream, chopped tomatoes, and cilantro.

- Enhanced jarred tomato sauce. If you don't have time to make Muscly Marinara (page 192), you can put the jarred sauce in a blender, add some canned lentils and a handful of spinach, and blend on high. If you have a high-powered blender, add a handful of cashews, too. Voilà! Serve on pasta or on store-bought polenta slices from a tube, fried up in a skillet.

- Field Roast vegan frankfurters cut up into very small pieces (only ages four and up to avoid choking), with ketchup spiked with a little bit of flax or hemp oil for extra omega-3s. Each frank has 21 grams of protein!

- Boxed vegan mac 'n' cheese with thawed freezer cubes of pureed pumpkin, squash, carrot, or sweet potato mixed in.

- Dr. Praeger's frozen veggie burgers.

- Instant oatmeal packets with a dab of nut butter and an extra splash of nondairy milk.

- Store-bought pancake mix made with nondairy milk and a third of a banana, mashed, in place of an egg. Check the ingredients on the pancake mix; many are vegan, but some are not.

PACKING LUNCHES
AND MEALS ON-THE-GO

Here are a bunch of options for packing school lunches and other
meals. All options are plant-based and can be peanut-free!

MAINS

- Baby Mac-o'-Lantern and Cheeze (page 82), with salt
- Baked Potato, a Dozen Ways (page 183)
- Black Bean–Tofu Burrito (page 181)
- Burrito made with beans, avocado, and salsa or Nacho Cashew Cheese Sauce (page 195)
- Chickpea–Sweet Potato Croquettes (page 93)
- Cinnamon raisin English muffin with vegan cream cheese and Berry Chia Jam (page 198)
- Clean-Out-the-Fridge Burgers (page 179)
- Cold sesame noodles
- English muffin mini pizza
- Falafel in a pita with veggies and tahini
- Fam-Fave Pizza (page 171)
- Favorite Veggie Risotto (page 166)
- Homemade or store-bought baked tofu (so many flavors), cut into sticks
- Hummus whole-grain cracker sandwiches
- Hummus wrap or hummus in a pita with veggies
- Khichdi (page 84)
- Kiddie Quesadillas (page 178)
- Laura's Lovely Lentils (page 152)
- Lo mein
- Magic Beans (page 167)

- Mashed chickpea, mayo, and nooch sandwich
- Pancakes with maple syrup on the side
- Pasta with Gween Sauce (page 190), Muscly Marinara (page 192), or Mac-o'-Lantern and Cheeze Sauce (page 191)
- Roasted Herbed Chickpeas (page 143)
- Sneaky Grilled Cheese (page 174) with Muscly Marinara (page 192)
- Stir-fried tofu and veggies over rice
- Store-bought veggie or black bean burger
- Sunflower seed butter tortilla wraps with a banana inside, cut into segments
- Sunnybutter Sammies (page 164)
- Tempeh Tacos (page 176)
- Tofu Dill Bites (page 173)
- Tofu Scramble (page 89)
- Tofu Sticks (page 168) with Peanutty Dipping Sauce (page 201, all-tahini variation)
- Vegan turkey sandwiches, made with vegan cheese and vegan mayo
- Veggie dumplings and veggie sushi
- White Bean Wonder Waffles (page 112), cut into sticks, with maple syrup
- Whole-grain bagel with vegan cream cheese, cucumber, and tomato

Try for Two

SNACKS AND SIDES

Veggies

- Baby carrots or carrot sticks
- Baked Kale Chips (page 131)
- Bell pepper spears
- Broccoli florets or Brilliant Broccoli (page 161)
- Broccoli Heart and Carrot Sticks (page 130) with Cashew Chive Spread (page 196) or hummus
- Celery, plain or filled with nut or sunflower seed butter or vegan cream cheese
- Cherry tomatoes
- Corn
- Cucumber slices or "sandwiches" (hummus or cream cheese between cucumber slices)
- Edamame
- Frozen peas
- Jessie's One and Only Guacamole (page 158) with tortilla chips or plantain chips
- Mini salad with dressing on the side
- Noochy Cauliflower Bites (page 159)
- Olives or pickles
- Seaweed snack sheets, like those from SeaSnax
- Shredded cabbage, with or without dressing
- Spring rolls
- Sugar snap peas
- Sweet potato hash browns or tater tots
- Sweet Potato Wedges (page 94)

Mix 'n' match

Fruit

- Apple slices, plain or with Caramel Sauce (page 200), if almonds are allowed
- Ayla's Banana-Mango Pudding (page 71)
- Banana with a message or picture on the peel
- Berries
- Canned peaches
- Clementine or mandarin segments
- Dried cherries, cranberries, or raisins (no-sugar-added)
- Fresh or canned pineapple chunks
- Fresh or dried apple, apricot, fig, mango, papaya
- Fruit leather or dehydrated fruit
- Goji berries
- Grapes
- Kiwi chunks, quartered
- Melon chunks
- Orange "smiles" (slices)
- Peach or plum slices or chunks
- Pitted cherries
- Pomegranate seeds

Continued

More snacks!

Miscellaneous

- Cashews or almonds, if tree nuts are allowed and if the child is age four or above
- Coconut chips (unsweetned)
- Granola
- Granola bars (MadeGood brand is school-safe)
- Lara bars (check for nuts)
- Mini pretzels (spelt ones often have more protein and iron than regular pretzels)
- Nondairy yogurt
- Peeled and cooked chestnuts
- Popcorn (age four or above), sprinkled with nutritional yeast or Vegan Parm Sprinkle (page 186)
- Seeds (pumpkin, sesame, or sunflower)
- Sesame sticks
- Snapea Crisps
- Soy yogurt
- Trail mix (dried fruit mixed with hulled pumpkin seeds or sunflower seeds)

Maybe a treat!

SWEETER SNACKS

- Annie's Bunny Grahams (not the honey flavor)
- Apple slices and Caramel Sauce (page 200), if almonds are allowed
- Caramel Corn (page 132)
- Chia Seed Pudding (page 137)
- Chocolate Cherry Chia Muffins (page 134), if almonds are allowed
- Chocolate Chip Banana Muffins (page 133)
- Chocolate Chip "Toohini" Cookies (page 210)
- Chocolate-covered chickpeas, blueberries, or banana
- Dessert hummus
- Dried fruit strips
- Dried papaya spears
- Fig cookies
- Four Seasons Fruit Crumble (page 208)
- Fudgy Nut-Free Energy Bites (page 138)
- Graham crackers (honey-free)
- Iron Sink Cookies (page 214)
- Orangutan-Approved Chocolate-Hazelnut Spread (page 199), if nuts are allowed, on crackers
- Simple Stuffed Date Halves (page 140)
- Snacky Snakes (page 139), nut-free version for nut-free schools
- Sweet Potato Spelt Biscuits (page 157)
- Vegan dark chocolate chips or chocolate square

Part One

OH, BABY!

You're here! You've made it through enough sleepless nights that now you're contemplating the next chapter in your baby's life: eating solid foods. So precious, so exciting, so messy. We hope you will have a camera on hand to capture your baby with her face, hair, and bib covered in ooey-gooey delights.

In the meantime, we'll try to answer some questions that new parents may have about starting solids. We'll share what the official guidelines are, leaning on recommendations from the American Academy of Pediatrics (AAP) and the *Nutrition Care Manual* of the Academy of Nutrition and Dietetics, the largest organization of nutrition professionals in the United States. We also acknowledge that vegan parents tend to think outside the box when it comes to feeding themselves and their families and may have special considerations, so we'll touch upon some of the less-mainstream ways of doing things as well.

WHEN AND WHAT AND HOW TO START

Maybe you've heard of parents feeding their babies solid foods at four months, five months, or six months. When's the right time to start?

The AAP recommends exclusive breastfeeding for the first six months. Some babies may be developmentally ready for solid foods a little before this—at around five months. Babies who were premature may need more than six months before they are ready for solid foods.

Signs of readiness

- She can hold her head up with solid head control while sitting in a high chair or baby seat.

- He seems interested in food and reaches for your food. If he opens his mouth when food comes in his direction, he might be telling you he's ready.

- She has the tongue dexterity to move food from her mouth to her throat to swallow. If she pushes the food out with her tongue, you might want to thin the food with breast milk or formula and try again. If she doesn't seem to be getting used to it, let it go for a few days or a week and then try again.

- He's doubled his birth weight and weighs 13 pounds or more.

- Some, but not all, studies have found that introducing wheat by five and a half months may reduce a child's risk of developing a wheat allergy. For this reason, and upon her pediatrician's recommendation, Marisa introduced her babies to wheat via multigrain baby cereal at five and a half months.

Where to Begin

The AAP states that it doesn't matter which solid foods you start with, as long as new foods are introduced one at a time, with an observation interval between each. They recommend starting out by feeding your baby one new food and waiting three to five days before introducing the next new food. Eventually you work up from one meal a day to three meals a day with a snack.

In the three to five days between each new food exposure, watch your child for any signs or symptoms of an allergic reaction or sensitivity. The waiting period helps you determine which new food might have caused the reaction; conversely, if you introduced two new foods at once and your baby had an allergic reaction, you won't know which of the two new foods caused it. Note that an allergic reaction usually won't occur upon first exposure to the allergen—after subsequent exposures, the body develops an immune response to the allergen and your child will likely display symptoms. These symptoms can include diarrhea, rash, or vomiting. If any of these occur, consult your pediatrician and do not introduce any new foods until the reaction has subsided and the doctor has given the go-ahead.

Allergenic Foods

Not long ago, the thinking was to limit babies' exposure to particularly allergenic foods such as peanuts until after their first year. However, according to the AAP, evidence now indicates that waiting that long might increase a child's chances of developing an allergy, so they recommend exposing babies to allergenic foods in safe ways (not giving them whole peanuts, for example) at closer to six months. Babies should have had some prior experience with solid foods to make sure they're ready to take on solids before introducing peanut products. There are some situations where medical supervision is needed when introducing peanut products (see page 25).

Our PBJ Smoothie Bowl (page 117) prepared without the optional Tutti-Frutti Sprinkle is a great way to expose babies to peanut butter (just make sure they are exposed to the other ingredients in the smoothie bowl first).

Other prevalent allergenic plant foods include tree nuts, wheat, soy, and sesame.

Starting with Cereals

Traditionally, American parents have started with single-grain infant cereals like rice cereal, then moved on to other cereals such as oat and multigrain. One advantage to this is that by six months, babies' natural iron stores are low, and iron-fortified baby cereals provide much-needed iron. The RDA for iron is especially high for six-to-twelve-month-olds: 11 milligrams, as opposed to 7 milligrams for one-to-three-year-olds. Since they're also eating fewer calories at six to twelve months than at one to three years, making sure they get enough iron is especially challenging. Iron-fortified infant cereals have been shown to be as effective as iron supplements at maintaining iron levels and preventing iron deficiency anemia. The AAP says breastfed infants should start taking a daily iron supplement at four months and continue the supplement until solid foods containing iron are introduced.

We've included recipes for purees that do contain a bit of iron—including a lentil puree, a bean puree, and a spinach puree—but on their own, these will not provide enough iron, so fortified cereals and/or supplements are recommended to fill the gap.

Mix the cereal with enough breast milk or formula to give it a soupy consistency. Start with 1 tablespoon on day 1, working up to 4 tablespoons per serving over time.

Rice cereal is a popular cereal to start with in the United States because of its mild flavor, smooth texture, and digestibility. But due to concerns about arsenic in rice, the AAP and the USDA recommend incorporating a variety of grains in infants' diets. Iron-fortified oat, multigrain, and barley cereals are easy to find, and we include a recipe for a (nonfortified) oat cereal on page 63.

Starting with Fruit, Veggie, and Bean Purees

In the United States, apple, pear, and peach purees are popular first foods. You can start out with just 1 tablespoon and increase the amount each day. Combining purees with iron-fortified cereals will lend much-needed iron to your baby's diet, or you can continue to supplement with iron.

Some parents choose to start with vegetable purees to get babies accustomed to those flavors early on. That makes sense, right? The thinking is that if babies start eating veggies early, they'll continue to happily eat veggies later on. The AAP insists that research does not bear this out, however. Breastfed babies are exposed to various flavors through breast milk, and acceptance of veggies does not change if fruits are introduced first. But we say the more veggies, the better, so if any vegucated parents want to go that route, we thoroughly approve! Squash, avocado, sweet potato, pumpkin, and carrot are popular first veggie purees.

While fruit and veggie purees are popular starter foods, there's no reason your baby can't start with a bean or legume puree. In fact, the Academy of Nutrition and Dietetics considers protein-rich beans and legumes, as well as iron- and zinc-fortified infant cereals, "ideal" first foods.

Starting with Finger Foods/ Baby-Led Weaning

Baby-led weaning (BLW) has become popular in recent years. You can't peruse any online parenting groups without reading "She eats what we eat." This is not really a revolutionary idea,

because babies have been eating small bits of their parents' meals for thousands of years. The appeal for many parents is that they don't need to give babies food that is different from theirs.

"Baby-led weaning" was coined in the United Kingdom by Gill Rapley, coauthor, with Tracey Murkett, of the 2008 book *Baby-Led Weaning: The Essential Guide to Introducing Solid Foods and Helping Your Baby to Grow Up a Happy and Confident Eater*. Instead of starting babies on spoon-feeding between four and six months, you exclusively breastfeed until they are six months, then have them join the family at mealtimes and offer them foods that they can grasp and feed to themselves. The idea was to take the stress away from feeding babies, giving them more control over what and how much they eat, and to make the whole food-introduction process more rewarding for parents and babies alike.

Choking Risks

Rapley assures parents that finger foods have been recommended to babies as part of a food-introduction regimen that includes purees anyway, so there is no higher risk of choking for babies whose parents choose to skip purees.

What Does the Science Say?

Because BLW is a relatively new concept, there isn't a ton of research on it yet, and the studies that have been done were smaller. One of the most prolific researchers of BLW is Amy Brown, professor of Public Health and Policy Studies at Swansea University in the UK. Based on her research, she concluded, "The baby-led approach has a lot of potential benefits, in part because of the healthy eating practices it encourages. Research shows us that if parents are following a baby-led approach they are more likely to delay introducing solid foods until around six months, to offer babies a wide variety of different foods to try, to avoid too many commercial products that can be high in sugar and, importantly, let their baby eat at their own pace, rather than encouraging them to finish a portion. Aspects of baby-led weaning such as allowing babies to handle and explore their food and to join in family mealtimes with everyone else are also important stages of learning to eat socially. All these factors together give babies an excellent start toward eating well throughout childhood and beyond."

To date, there has been no research on vegan babies whose parents practiced BLW. An observational study in 2016 indicated that iron consumption of babies following BLW was less than half that of infants following traditional spoon-feeding, compounding nutritionists' concerns that iron may be an issue.

In one 2018 study that tried to address this issue, researchers instructed parents on using a modified version of BLW that stressed the importance of including iron-rich food such as fortified infant cereal or red meat with every meal. Iron levels were measured and were considered adequate. But if red meat is out of the question, can babies feed themselves enough cereal to reach the 11 milligram RDA for iron? What about beans, spinach, and legumes?

Iron amounts in ¼ cup of the following foods:

Tofu = 3.3 milligrams

Lentils = 1.65 milligrams

Spinach = 1.6 milligrams

Kidney beans = 1.3 milligrams

Chickpeas = 1.2 milligrams

Navy beans, soybeans, lima beans, black-eyed peas = 1.1 milligrams

Given that the RDA for six-to-twelve-month-olds is 11 milligrams, continuing iron supplementation would be wise for those who want to try BLW. See page 16 for more information about iron.

While the AAP has not yet come out with an official position on baby-led weaning, it does approve of self-feeding for babies who are developmentally ready to sit up on their own and bring food to their mouths. The AAP stipulates that foods given to babies should be soft and cut into small pieces for ease of swallowing without the risk of choking.

Alexandra Caspero Lenz and Whitney English Tabaie, authors of the plant-based baby-led weaning e-book *First Bites*, say "a good rule is that food should be soft enough to squish between your pointer finger and thumb."

Popular first finger foods for BLW:

Ripe avocado or ripe banana

Well-steamed broccoli florets or carrot sticks

Steamed or roasted zucchini or summer squash

Well-cooked potatoes, peas, or pasta

Toast sticks

Sticks of raw watermelon, seeded

Bite-size pieces of soft very ripe mango

Shards of soft ripe strawberries and cut-up raspberries

Apple or pear, peeled, cored, steamed until very soft, and cut into spears

Sweet Potato Wedges (page 94)

Well-cooked beets

HOW TO USE THIS BOOK IF YOU ARE BABY-LED WEANING

Parents tend to use the term "baby-led weaning" loosely. For some it means exclusively offering finger foods, but for many, it means offering a majority of finger foods but also some textured purees or mashed foods that babies can feed themselves—in other words, rake up with their hands and bring to their mouths. Recipe contributor Lisa Pitman uses ground oats in her recipe for Isla's Magic Oats (page 63) and suggests serving it as a base for mashed fruits and veggies.

The next two chapters contain recipes for purees that babies can certainly explore with their hands and mouths. Just serve them with a textured grain or blend the food enough so that the puree retains some texture. If you'd rather not do purees at all, you can follow the recipe to steam the food, allow it to cool, then cut it into spears or other graspable shapes instead of pureeing it as directed.

The Play with Your Food chapter (page 75) contains meals that babies can rake up with their hands and put in their mouths. You will notice a lot of recipes with several ingredients, so you can start with one ingredient in the recipe and work up to more each time you make it.

The Good Grub to Grab chapter (page 87) contains foods ideally shaped for good little grabbers.

Both the Play with Your Food and Good Grub to Grab chapters contain recipes that older kids and even parents can enjoy. Just keep baby's portions salt-free and season portions for older kids and adults with salt as desired (or not at all, if that's your preference).

Many of the recipes for toddlers and older kids contain great meal options for BLW babies. Again, we recommend preparing the meal or side dish without salt, portioning some out for baby, then seasoning portions for older kids and adults with salt as desired.

Foods to avoid in baby's first year:

Added sugar

Added salt

Processed foods

Fried foods

Honey (which many vegans avoid anyway)

Fruit juices

Caffeinated drinks

_____

The salt question can be particularly bothersome because it would simplify our lives so much if our babies could just eat what we eat. Many families do that anyway, but studies have shown that babies exposed to salt early develop a preference for it as infants and preschoolers. This preference could lead to health problems as they get older. Because babies haven't been exposed to high-sodium foods when they start eating solid foods, they don't expect food to taste salty. They may be better able to appreciate the real flavor of the food than those of us who "need" salt in our meals.

Babies who eat more ready-to-eat store-bought and processed foods may also have increased risk of health problems later. In one study, children, as young as seven and a half, who had eaten more ready-made and processed foods as infants had higher blood pressure than those who had eaten a healthier diet with fewer of these foods.

Choking hazards to avoid:

Nuts, unless finely ground or blended and added to other foods

Seeds, unless finely ground or blended and added to other foods

Peanut butter or other nut/seed butters unless mixed into other foods. Avoid nut or seed butters by the spoonful or on crackers or bread.

Hard apples or apple chunks

Raw carrots or other hard vegetables

Whole grapes

Popcorn

Vegan hot dogs

Variety Rules

Babies definitely exhibit their own taste preferences, but don't let that hold you back. As Reed Mangels explained on page 24, it takes ten to fifteen exposures (and sometimes more) for a little one to actually develop a liking for a food. Marixsa Watson, UK-based vegan mum and author of *More Fruit and Veg, Please*, reminds readers that "Whatever food was discounted should be reintroduced at a later date because taste buds do change and evolve over time. My son loved broccoli puree, but at first did not like the texture of the florets. When I tried the second time, he loved it and now will even eat it raw."

Studies show that the more foods babies are exposed to in their first year, the more likely they are to try new foods as toddlers, an age when neophobia, the fear of new or unfamiliar things, becomes an issue. Picky eating is the pits, so expose them to as many healthy plant foods in various flavors, colors, and textures as you can.

The following chapter contains recipes for single-taste purees and cereals. Exposing foods as single tastes is helpful not only in determining if your child has a sensitivity or allergy to a particular food, but also for babies to learn to appreciate the flavors of individual foods.

We don't include recipes for iron-fortified store-bought infant cereals because you can simply follow the directions on the container. Once you have fed your baby the cereal on its own, feel free to combine the cereal with a single-taste puree. Apple, pear, peach, sweet potato, and squash are popular first cereal companions, but there's no reason you can't feed your baby lentil or bean purees with a grain cereal.

Top tips for baby's first bites

- Set baby on your lap or in a high chair.

- If you're starting with purees or cereals, make them really thin, then gradually make them thicker or chunkier.

- If you're doing BLW, start with foods that are easy for her to pick up, like thick sticks or long strips, then gradually introduce new shapes and textures.

- Dab new foods on your baby's lips first and let him lick it off.

- Let her touch/play with the food and/ or the spoon. Sometimes it helps to give her a spoon to play with while you feed her with a separate spoon.

- Let him decide how much to eat and when he's done. Be responsive to his cues and never force him to eat when he doesn't want to.

- Never leave her alone with food. Eat your meal with her if you can; keep the atmosphere light, and be prepared that she may be more interested in what's on your plate than hers.

- Offer him water to drink during meals.

- Have fun, and take pictures!

HELPFUL SAMPLE WEEKLY MENUS

Our nutritionist, Reed Mangels, put together the following weekly menus that use the recipes in the four baby food chapters to show how the baby's weekly menu might evolve over time to incorporate more foods.

Each of these charts follows a more conventional baby feeding approach, beginning with purees and cereals and building up to more textured foods and finger foods. They serve as examples of a balanced vegan baby's diet to be used as guidelines or inspiration for your own menus.

Please note that the charts reflect what your baby might be eating toward the end of the given month or month range. They assume that many of the featured foods have already been introduced to expose the baby to a new food 3 to 5 days in a row to look for signs of an allergic reaction or sensitivity. If at any time you believe that your baby has a reaction to a food with symptoms such as diarrhea, a rash, or vomiting, talk with your baby's doctor about whether or not that food needs to be avoided.

Infants should continue to be fed breast milk/formula on demand. Exclusively bottle-fed infants typically take in 24 to 32 ounces of formula or pumped breast milk at 6 to 8 months and about 24 ounces at 9 to 12 months. Milk feedings are not included in the meal plan since timing and amount will vary for each infant.

The timing of each snack (whether mid-morning, mid-afternoon, or both) will depend on nap times and on length of time between meals.

WEEKLY MENU
FOR A 6-MONTH-OLD*

	Breakfast	Dinner
Monday	Peach Puree Baby oat cereal mixed with breast milk or infant formula	Sweet Pea Puree Baby multigrain cereal mixed with breast milk or infant formula
Tuesday	Apple Puree Baby barley cereal mixed with breast milk or infant formula	Sweet Pea Puree Baby oat cereal mixed with breast milk or infant formula
Wednesday	Peach Puree Baby multigrain cereal mixed with breast milk or infant formula	Sweet Pea Puree Baby barley cereal mixed with breast milk or infant formula
Thursday	Apple Puree Baby oat cereal mixed with breast milk or infant formula	Sweet Pea Puree Baby multigrain cereal mixed with breast milk or infant formula
Friday	Peach Puree Baby barley cereal mixed with breast milk or infant formula	Butternut Squash Puree Lentil Puree Baby oat cereal mixed with breast milk or infant formula
Saturday	Apple Puree Baby multigrain cereal mixed with breast milk or infant formula	Butternut Squash Puree Lentil Puree Baby barley cereal mixed with breast milk or infant formula
Sunday	Peach Puree Baby oat cereal mixed with breast milk or infant formula	Butternut Squash Puree Lentil Puree Baby multigrain cereal mixed with breast milk or infant formula

*Sample menu is intended for the end of the first month of introducing solid food and assumes you have already introduced all these foods except for Sweet Pea Puree and Lentil Puree, which you are introducing here.

WEEKLY MENU
FOR A 7-MONTH-OLD*

	Breakfast	Lunch	Snack	Dinner
Monday	Just Peachy Cereal	Apricot and White Bean Carrot Puree	Apple Puree	Baby Mushroom-Walnut Pâté Puree Baby multigrain cereal mixed with breast milk or infant formula
Tuesday	Baby oat cereal mixed with breast milk or infant formula Peach Puree	Apricot and White Bean	Apple Puree	Cinnamon—Sweet Potato Oats Lentil Puree
Wednesday	Apple Puree Baby barley cereal mixed with breast milk or infant formula	Avocado for Your Sweet Pea Apricot and White Bean	Blueberry Puree	Berries-and-Basil Barley with Beans
Thursday	Peas Porridge Hot	Baby Mushroom-Walnut Pâté Puree Spinach Puree	Baby oat cereal mixed with breast milk or infant formula	Apricot and White Bean Butternut Squash Puree
Friday	Baby multigrain cereal mixed with breast milk or infant formula Dried Apricot (or Prune) Puree	Broccoli Pear Lentil Puree	Blueberry Puree	Cinnamon—Sweet Potato Oats Baby Mushroom-Walnut Pâté Puree
Saturday	Peas Porridge Hot	Apricot and White Bean Spinach Puree	Blueberry Puree	Berries-and-Basil Barley with Beans
Sunday	Baby oat cereal mixed with breast milk or infant formula Apple Puree	Butternut Squash Puree Apricot and White Bean	Blueberry Puree	Peas Porridge Hot Bean Puree

*Sample menu is intended for the end of the seventh month and assumes you have already introduced all these foods except for apricots in Apricot and White Bean and blueberries, which you are introducing here.

WEEKLY MENU FOR A 9-TO-12-MONTH-OLD

	Breakfast	Lunch	Snack	Dinner
Monday	Top o' the Morning Green Power Pancakes	Dahlia's Baby Dal Blueberry Powerhouse Pudding	Teething Rusks	Southwestern Baby Bowl Sweet Potato Wedges
Tuesday	Just Peachy Cereal	Baby Mushroom-Walnut Pâté Puree Small pieces of whole-grain toast or bread Soft ripe mango pieces	Top o' the Morning Green Power Pancakes	Khichdi
Wednesday	Baby multigrain cereal mixed with breast milk or infant formula Sliced ripe banana	Tofu Scramble Sweet Potato Wedges Steamed apple slices	Avocado Toast Fingers with Nooch	Smashed White Beans with Onion and Herbs Small pieces of whole-grain toast or bread Green Beans and Almond Cream
Thursday	Baby barley cereal mixed with breast milk or infant formula Apple Puree	Smashed White Beans with Onion and Herbs Creamed Kale Ayla's Banana-Mango Pudding	Teething Rusks	Baby Guacabowlie Quinoa
Friday	Top o' the Morning Green Power Pancakes	Khichdi	Seeded watermelon cubes	Chickpea–Sweet Potato Croquettes Cashew Creamed Kale
Saturday	Baby oat cereal mixed with breast milk or infant formula Sliced strawberries	Baby Guacabowlie Sliced ripe banana	Steamed diced sweet potato	Tofu Scramble Avocado Toast Fingers with Nooch Steamed broccoli florets
Sunday	Just Peachy Cereal	Chickpea–Sweet Potato Croquettes Seeded watermelon cubes	Teething Rusks	Baby Mac-o'-Lantern and Cheeze

YUMMY IN YOUR
TINY TUMMY

APPLE PUREE

PEAR PUREE

PEACH PUREE

CARROT PUREE

SWEET PEA PUREE

BROCCOLI PUREE

SWEET POTATO PUREE

BUTTERNUT SQUASH PUREE

BEAN PUREE

LENTIL PUREE

BLUEBERRY PUREE

STRAWBERRY PUREE

SPINACH PUREE

DRIED APRICOT (OR PRUNE) PUREE

ISLA'S MAGIC OATS

STEAMING AND PUREEING BASICS

In this chapter, you will find simple single-taste purees to start baby out with, that you can then use for mixing in the next chapter.

For all steamed purees you can follow the same method:

Fill a small to medium pot with about 1 inch of water. Place a steamer basket in the pot, cover the pot, and bring the water to a simmer over high heat, then adjust heat as needed to keep it at a simmer.

While the water is warming up, wash, peel, core or pit (if necessary), and chop the fruit or vegetable. The smaller the pieces, the faster they will cook.

Put the fruit or vegetable in the steamer basket and cover the pot again. Steam the fruit or vegetable until it is soft enough that a fork slides through it easily. Remove from the heat and let cool.

Transfer the fruit or veg to a blender and blend until very smooth, adding water from the pot, breast milk, or formula to thin the puree until it reaches the desired consistency, which will be thinner and soupier for newer eaters and thicker and chunkier for more experienced eaters.

STORAGE BASICS

Most purees will keep in an airtight container in the fridge for 2 to 3 days, but there are some exceptions; avocado and spinach purees, for example, taste best when consumed fresh. Fresh foods spoil more quickly than canned and jarred foods because cans and jars are processed to kill any bacteria inside. Before feeding your baby foods that have been refrigerated for more than a couple of days, it's a good idea to smell or taste it yourself first. To cut down on bacterial growth in the food, don't feed baby directly from the storage container; instead, portion out a serving in a separate dish. Some purees will thicken in the fridge, so you can just add water to thin when needed.

Food that won't get eaten within 2 to 3 days can be portioned into ice cube trays or baby-food storage trays and frozen overnight. Transfer the frozen cubes to resealable freezer bags, use a permanent marker to label the bags with their contents and the date, and return them to the freezer. Frozen purees will keep for up to 3 months.

Options for reheating a frozen puree:

Place it in an airtight container in the fridge to thaw overnight.

Put it in a warm water bath for 15 to 20 minutes, switching out the water periodically as it cools.

Put enough frozen cubes for one serving in a microwave-safe container and microwave it for 15 seconds, adding more seconds in small increments as needed, but do be sure to stir it well afterwards to ensure there are no hot spots.

Place the frozen cubes in a saucepan over low heat until thawed. Liquid in the puree can evaporate as it reheats and cause it to thicken more than you like; if this happens, just stir in some water until the desired consistency is reached.

APPLE PUREE

MAKES ABOUT ¾ CUP

Apple puree is a great way to introduce your baby to the mild, sweet taste of fruit. Apples supply potassium and some vitamin C.

Peel, core, and chop **3 sweet red apples**, such as Fuji, Gala, Honeycrisp, McIntosh, Macoun, or Pink Lady. Following the instructions on page 58, steam the apples for 10 to 15 minutes, then let cool and blend as directed.

PEAR PUREE

MAKES ABOUT 1 CUP

This fruity puree introduces your baby to pears, which are a good source of potassium, a mineral that supports kidney and muscle function.

Peel, core, and chop **2 fresh pears**. If they are very soft, ripe, and juicy, you might not need to steam them at all before pureeing them; just put them in the blender and puree. If they are still firm, follow the instructions on page 58 and steam the pears for 4 to 8 minutes, then let cool and blend as directed.

PEACH PUREE

MAKES 1 CUP

Peaches, like other deep orange fruits, are good sources of vitamin A and potassium. Introduce them early, and it's likely that peaches will be one of your little one's favorites.

Peel, pit and chop **3 fresh peaches**. If they are super ripe and soft, you might not need to steam them at all before pureeing; just put them in the blender and puree. If they are still somewhat firm, follow the instructions on page 58 and steam the peaches for 3 to 6 minutes, then let cool and blend as directed.

> Variation **When peaches are in season, you can freeze slices for use later when they're not. To use them, steam 2½ frozen peach slices for 12 to 15 minutes, then let cool and blend as directed.**

CARROT PUREE

MAKES 1 CUP

A 2-tablespoon serving of this puree has more than half the vitamin A your baby needs for the day. Vitamin A is important for eye health and a strong immune system.

Following the instructions on page 58, steam **4 medium carrots** for 12 to 15 minutes, then let cool and blend as directed.

SWEET PEA PUREE

MAKES 1 CUP

A 2-tablespoon serving of sweet pea puree delivers more than one-quarter of the folate and about 15 percent of the zinc that your baby needs daily for growth and development.

Shell about **2 pounds of fresh peas** in the pods to make 2 cups, or use 2 cups frozen sweet peas. Following the instructions on page 58, steam the peas for 10 to 12 minutes, then let cool and blend as directed.

BROCCOLI PUREE

MAKES 1 CUP

A couple of tablespoons of this puree will help your baby get acquainted with the taste of broccoli, a nutrient-filled vegetable. Those 2 tablespoons also supply at least 10 percent of the vitamin C, potassium, riboflavin, and folate that a six-to-twelve-month-old needs daily.

Following the instructions on page 58, steam **3 cups broccoli florets** for 15 to 18 minutes, then let cool and blend as directed.

SWEET POTATO PUREE

MAKES 1 CUP

Just a 2-tablespoon serving of sweet potato puree supplies more than half the vitamin A an infant needs each day, plus at least 10 percent of baby's RDA of both potassium and magnesium.

Peel and chop **2 small sweet potatoes**. Following the instructions on page 58, steam for 12 to 15 minutes, then let cool and blend as directed.

BUTTERNUT SQUASH PUREE

MAKES ABOUT 2 CUPS

Butternut squash is a good introduction to the important orange vegetables, and a 2-tablespoon serving of this puree packs in 10 percent of the vitamin A your baby needs daily. Roasting the squash lends a lovely flavor and enhances its sweetness, but if you're pinched for time, you can buy prechopped fresh or frozen butternut squash and steam it instead.

Preheat the oven to 400°F. Cut off the stem of **1 medium butternut squash**, then halve the squash lengthwise and scoop out the seeds. Pour enough water into a baking pan or rimmed baking sheet to cover the bottom. Place the squash halves cut-side down in the pan. Roast until tender, about 40 minutes, then remove from the oven and let cool. Scoop out the squash seeds and discard or compost them, then scoop the flesh of the squash into a blender (discard/compost the skins), and blend as instructed on page 58.

Variation Alternatively, steam 2 cups chopped fresh or frozen butternut squash for 10 to 14 minutes, then let cool and blend as directed. (Makes 1 cup puree.)

BEAN PUREE

MAKES ABOUT 1 CUP

Our freezer always had a stash of chickpea puree and cannellini bean puree, but any bean will do. Just 1½ tablespoons of this puree will provide about 20 percent of your baby's daily protein needs, more than 10 percent of the RDA for zinc, and more than half the RDA for folate, a vitamin that is involved in growth and development.

Drain and rinse **1 (15-ounce) can of beans** (preferably no salt added or reduced sodium). Transfer the beans to a blender and blend until smooth. Add water, breast milk, or formula to reach the desired consistency.

LENTIL PUREE

MAKES ABOUT 1 CUP

A 1½-tablespoon serving of lentil puree supplies about 20 percent of the protein and folate and 10 percent of the zinc, thiamine, and vitamin B₆ an infant needs each day.

In a medium pot, bring 1 cup water to a boil over high heat. Add ½ **cup dried split red lentils** and stir. Cover the pot with the lid ajar and return the water to a boil, then reduce the heat to low. Simmer the lentils, stirring occasionally, until tender, 12 to 15 minutes. If they start to dry out, add a little water. Remove from the heat, let cool, then blend as directed on page 58.

Lentils can thicken more when stored in the fridge; add a little water when you reheat them to return them to the desired consistency.

BLUEBERRY PUREE

MAKES ABOUT 1 CUP

This delightful puree will introduce your baby to blueberries—a good source of vitamin C and potassium, as well as antioxidants, including anthocyanin.

If your blueberries are ripe, there's no need to steam them—just put **2 cups blueberries** in the blender and puree. If they are not ripe or if you're using frozen berries, follow the instructions on page 58 and steam them for 3 to 5 minutes, then let cool and blend.

> Variation Blueberry-Basil Puree: For more advanced eaters, add 2 fresh basil leaves to the blender before pureeing the blueberries to give the puree a sophisticated summery twist.

STRAWBERRY PUREE

MAKES 1 CUP

A third of your baby's daily vitamin C requirement is in a 1½-tablespoon serving of this fruity puree. Vitamin C helps your baby absorb iron from foods like lentil puree (at left) and bean puree (see page 61).

Hull and halve **2 cups fresh strawberries**. If they are ripe, there's no need to steam them— just put them in the blender and puree. If they are underripe or if you're using frozen berries, follow the instructions on page 58 and steam them for 3 to 5 minutes, then let cool and blend as directed.

SPINACH PUREE

MAKES ⅔ CUP

Spinach lends a bit of iron to any puree, and the vitamin C in this puree helps make sure that iron is absorbed. Using a high-powered blender such as a Vitamix will ensure that the puree is nice and smooth.

Spinach cooks down—steaming a whole 5-ounce package of baby spinach will yield only ⅔ cup puree, so if you want to make more than that for your freezer stash, steam multiple batches.

Remove the tough stems from **8 ounces of regular (not baby) spinach** (otherwise, use one 5-ounce package of baby spinach—no need to remove any stems). Following the instructions on page 58, steam the spinach for 4 to 6 minutes, then let cool and blend.

DRIED APRICOT (OR PRUNE) PUREE

MAKES 1 CUP

This puree adds some sweetness to any dish. You can use this method to puree all kinds of dried fruit, from figs to prunes. (Prune puree comes in handy if your baby gets stopped up, which can happen sometimes when you introduce baby cereal to her diet.) A serving of apricot puree is a great way to supply potassium, an essential mineral, and 1½ tablespoons deliver more than 15 percent of the potassium your baby needs each day.

In a small pot, combine **1 cup dried apricots (or prunes)** and 1 cup water. Cover the pot and bring the water to a boil over high heat. Reduce the heat to maintain a simmer and cook until the apricots (or prunes) are tender, 8 to 10 minutes. Remove from the heat and let cool, then blend as directed on page 58.

> Note Because this puree has a higher (natural) sugar content, it won't freeze—the sugar lowers the freezing point of the puree, keeping it from solidifying. But that same higher sugar content helps to prevent spoilage, so you can store the puree in an airtight container in the fridge a bit longer than fresh fruit purees.

ISLA'S MAGIC OATS

See page 67 for a sweet potato and cinnamon version. A serving made with 2 tablespoons ground oats supplies 25 percent of the RDA for magnesium for a six-to-twelve-month-old. Unlike commercial infant cereals, this one doesn't provide much iron; if you plan to use this in place of those cereals, your baby may need an age-appropriate iron supplement (see page 16).

by Lisa Pitman

MAKES 1 CUP (4 TO 8 SERVINGS)

1 cup rolled oats

1 to 2 tablespoons boiling water, for serving

1 to 2 tablespoons mashed fruit or steamed vegetable, such as sweet potato or butternut squash, for serving (optional)

In a spice grinder or blender, grind the oats into a coarse powder. Transfer the oats to a jar, seal, and store at room temperature for up to a month. When ready to serve, portion out 1 to 2 tablespoons of the ground oats into a bowl and add an equal quantity of boiling water. Stir to combine, adding more boiling water if a smoother consistency is desired. Stir in the mashed fruit or vegetable, if desired. Let cool slightly before serving.

———

"These magical oats keep little ones coming back for more until you're scraping the bowl clean. They can be prepped ahead for meals on the go. They are a great base to introduce new flavors by adding mashed fruits and/or vegetables. Isla's favorites are banana or pear with a sprinkle of cinnamon."

—Lisa

STIR IT UP,
LITTLE DARLING

CINNAMON–SWEET POTATO OATS

JUST PEACHY CEREAL

CARROT APPLE

BROCCOLI PEAR

APRICOT AND WHITE BEAN

AVOCADO FOR YOUR SWEET PEA

PEAS PORRIDGE HOT

BERRIES-AND-BASIL BARLEY WITH BEANS

STRAWBERRY, SPINACH, AND APRICOT PUREE

LENTIL AND CARROT PUREE

AYLA'S BANANA-MANGO PUDDING

CREAMY COCONUT SQUASH

BLUEBERRY POWERHOUSE PUDDING

BABY MUSHROOM-WALNUT PÂTÉ PUREE

Now that you've got the basic purees down, this is your chance to get a little creative with your combinations. Maybe you've seen the baby food pouches at the store with all kinds of crazy flavor pairings going on that our parents sure as heck never tried on us. It's as if the strategists at the baby food companies got together in a conference room and dreamt up the kookiest combos: kale, kiwi, raisin, and amaranth? Perfect! Put it in a pouch!

What it does tell you is that the sky's the limit, and you can think outside the box—and outside the pouch—when making your own creations. We had fun dreaming up a few kooky combos ourselves, which we've interspersed among the classics in this chapter. We hope you use them as a jumping-off point for your own creations.

While the pouches are good inspiration, and handy when you're on the go, the ones that have gorgeous pictures of veggies and fruits on them are far more fruit than veggie. This might make babies like them more, which sells more pouches, but loading up on the fruit doesn't help babies acquire a taste for veggies. In fact, if you really want your baby to learn to enjoy veggies, you have to feed them just straight veggies sometimes.

Relying too much on puree pouches is not great for baby's development, either. Babies are born knowing how to suck, but they must learn to chew, push food to the backs of their mouths with their tongues, and swallow. If they are too used to the easy action of sucking down their food, they might develop an aversion to chewing textured foods.

In short, those pouches can be a lifesaver, but homemade puree mixes are better for baby, and they're clearly better for the environment, since those pouches are going straight to the landfill once baby's done. It's best to limit them to when you're on the go. If you'd like to save some money and some stress on the planet, you can buy reusable pouches and fill them with homemade baby food for when you're out and about.

CINNAMON–SWEET POTATO OATS

This sweet potato version of Isla's Magic Oats is seasoned with cinnamon and has one-third of the vitamin A that a baby needs in a day. Vitamin A helps the lungs, heart, kidneys, and other organs work properly.

MAKES 1 SERVING

2 tablespoons Isla's Magic Oats (page 63)

1 tablespoon Sweet Potato Puree (page 61)

Sprinkle of ground cinnamon (optional)

In a small bowl, stir together the oats, sweet potato, and cinnamon (if using). Let cool before serving.

JUST PEACHY CEREAL

This recipe makes a single serving for many babies and can supply more than 30 percent of the iron, zinc, and calcium that a six-to-twelve-month-old infant needs. To maximize nutrition, use a brand of baby cereal fortified with iron, calcium, and other nutrients.

MAKES 1 SERVING

2 tablespoons fortified multigrain baby cereal

3 tablespoons water, breast milk, or formula

2 tablespoons Peach Puree (page 59)

In a small bowl, stir together the cereal, water, and peach puree.

CARROT APPLE

This flavor duo is so beloved that it reappears as a juice in our Sips and Slurps chapter. Supplying more than half the daily vitamin A and 20 percent of the daily potassium that a baby needs, a 4-tablespoon serving of Carrot Apple helps to support baby's immune system, vision, and much more.

MAKES 1 SERVING

2 tablespoons Carrot Puree (page 59)

2 tablespoons Apple Puree (page 59)

In a small bowl, stir together the carrot and apple purees.

BROCCOLI PEAR

A perfect pear-ing! A 4-tablespoon serving of Broccoli Pear provides about 10 percent of the daily potassium and magnesium an older infant needs, as well as supplying vitamin C and folate.

MAKES 1 SERVING

2 tablespoons Broccoli Puree (page 61)

2 tablespoons Pear Puree (page 59)

In a small bowl, stir together the broccoli and pear purees.

APRICOT AND WHITE BEAN

Don't ask us why this funky combo works, but it does. A sprinkle of pumpkin pie spice instantly makes it dessert-y and autumnal. Four tablespoons of Apricot and White Bean supplies 75 percent of the folate, about 30 percent of the protein, and 10 percent of the iron and calcium that a baby needs in a day. All these nutrients help to support baby's growth and development.

MAKES 1 SERVING

2 tablespoons Dried Apricot Puree (page 63)

2 tablespoons Bean Puree (page 61), prepared with white beans

Sprinkle of pumpkin pie spice (optional)

In a small bowl, stir together the apricot and bean purees and the pumpkin pie spice (if using).

AVOCADO FOR YOUR SWEET PEA

This is like a really mild starter guacamole with a little bit of protein. A serving for six-to-twelve-month-olds (about 3 tablespoons) is an easy way to supply potassium (24 percent of the daily recommendation), zinc (15 percent), and vitamin E (more than 10 percent).

MAKES 5 TABLESPOONS (ABOUT 1½ SERVINGS)

¼ ripe avocado

2 tablespoons Sweet Pea Puree (page 59)

In a small bowl, combine the avocado and the pea puree and smash them together with a fork until any larger lumps of avocado are gone. Stir in the optional add-ins of your choice and serve immediately.

> Variation More advanced tasters might enjoy a bit of finely chopped cilantro, a pinch of onion powder, or a squeeze of lime juice.

PEAS PORRIDGE HOT

Okay, well, maybe not hot—just lukewarm, to be safe—but the idea is the same: yummy peas with a nutritious grain. Don't keep them in the pot for nine days, please. Fortified cereals are such a simple way to add iron to your baby's diet. This single-serving recipe has 40 percent of the iron a six-to-twelve-month-old needs in a day. It also weighs in with more than a third of the RDA of calcium, zinc, and B vitamins.

MAKES 1 SERVING

2 tablespoons fortified oat baby cereal

3 tablespoons water, breast milk, or formula

1 tablespoon Sweet Pea Puree (page 59)

In a small bowl, stir together the cereal, water, and sweet pea puree.

BERRIES-AND-BASIL BARLEY WITH BEANS

Is it bad to admit that many of our flavor combos are inspired by alliteration? Judge away, but this combo works. We love the sweet nuttiness and variation of barley cereal, if you can find it, but any fortified cereal will do. This recipe has plenty of B vitamins, too. Moving away from the Bs, a serving of this puree provides a quarter of a baby's daily iron requirements and 15 percent of the calcium and zinc that a six-to-ten-month-old needs in a day.

MAKES 1 SERVING

2 tablespoons iron-fortified barley baby cereal

3 tablespoons water, breast milk, or formula

1 tablespoon Blueberry-Basil Puree (see variation, page 62)

1 tablespoon Bean Puree (page 61)

In a small bowl, stir together the cereal, water, and blueberry and bean purees.

STRAWBERRY, SPINACH, AND APRICOT PUREE

The vibrant fruits and vegetables in this recipe make it a colorful way to add vitamins and minerals to your baby's meal. A 3-tablespoon serving supplies 30 percent of the vitamin C, 25 percent of the potassium, and 15 percent of the vitamin A that an older infant needs every day.

MAKES 1 SERVING

1 tablespoon Strawberry Puree (page 62)

1 tablespoon Spinach Puree (page 62)

1 tablespoon Dried Apricot Puree (page 63)

In a small bowl, stir together the strawberry, spinach, and apricot purees.

LENTIL AND CARROT PUREE

Carrots go so well with lentils. Thanks to the carrots, just 2 tablespoons of Lentil and Carrot Puree delivers 25 percent of the vitamin A that a six-to-twelve-month-old needs. And thanks to the lentils, one serving supplies more than 10 percent of the daily protein needed.

MAKES 1 SERVING

1 tablespoon Lentil Puree (page 62)

1 tablespoon Carrot Puree (page 59)

In a small bowl, stir together the lentil and carrot purees.

AYLA'S BANANA-MANGO PUDDING

This pudding is best if eaten fresh, but if you have some left over, feel free to freeze it in an ice pop mold for a healthy treat! A 2-tablespoon serving of this tropical pudding supplies about 15 percent of the vitamin B_6 that your baby needs every day. Vitamin B_6 plays a role in brain development.

by Tere Fox

MAKES 2 CUPS (16 SERVINGS)

1 mango, pitted and peeled, or 1 cup fresh mango slices

1½ ripe bananas

1 teaspoon hulled hemp seeds

Combine all the ingredients in a blender and blend until creamy. Portion out the quantity your baby will eat today and place it in a small bowl, then freeze the remainder in an ice pop mold (see headnote).

Variation For more advanced eaters, top the pudding with chopped banana from the remaining banana half, some chopped mango, or—a personal favorite in our house—fresh raspberries.

"Our children love to help create fresh fruit smoothies and puddings. They understand what nutrition is and get excited to combine new flavors."

—Tere

CREAMY COCONUT SQUASH

Thanks to the butternut squash, a 3-tablespoon serving of Creamy Coconut Squash supplies 15 percent of your baby's daily vitamin A. The cashews make it a good source of zinc, with 3 tablespoons of this puree clocking in at almost 20 percent of the recommended intake for your baby. The squash and cashews together mean each serving has a healthy dose of potassium (20 percent of baby's RDA).

If you don't have a high-speed blender like a Vitamix, you'll need to soak the cashews overnight, so be sure to plan ahead.

MAKES A LITTLE MORE THAN ¾ CUP (ABOUT 4 SERVINGS)

¼ cup cashews (see headnote)

¾ cup Butternut Squash Puree (page 61)

2 tablespoons coconut milk

If you've soaked your cashews, drain and rinse them. Combine all the ingredients in a blender with 2 tablespoons water and blend until smooth. Portion 3 tablespoons into a small bowl to serve now and store the remainder in an airtight container in the refrigerator for up to 3 days.

Variation For more advanced eaters, stir in ½ teaspoon garlic powder and ⅛ teaspoon ground cumin.

BLUEBERRY POWERHOUSE PUDDING

A 3-tablespoon serving of Blueberry Powerhouse Pudding has around 12 percent of an infant's daily zinc. It also provides more than a third of the daily requirement of magnesium.

by Kendra Fitzgerald

MAKES 2 CUPS (ABOUT 10 SERVINGS)

½ cup frozen chopped spinach

1 cup frozen blueberries

3 prunes

¼ cup Apple Puree (page 59) or unsweetened applesauce

5 tablespoons chia seeds

In a small pot, combine the spinach, blueberries, prunes, and ½ cup water and bring to a boil over high heat. Reduce the heat to medium and cook, stirring occasionally, until the blueberries and prunes are plump and soft, about 10 minutes. Remove from the heat and stir in the applesauce and chia seeds. Let stand for 10 minutes. Transfer the mixture to a blender or food processor and blend on high until completely smooth. Depending on your blender, you might need to add more water to reach the desired consistency.

"I came up with this recipe when my first son, Liam, was eight months old. He is now five, and his brother, Aidan, is two, and they both inhale this pudding like it's dessert. I feel great giving them as much as they want because it's loaded with nutrients. They love to help me blend it, and as soon as it's done blending, Liam always says, 'Mama! I want to EAT IT!'"

—Kendra

BABY MUSHROOM-WALNUT PÂTÉ PUREE

Marisa grew up eating pâtés, including liverwurst pâté, every summer while staying with family in Germany. She is delighted to have the chance to share her love of pâté with her kids, leaving the "wurst" part out of it: the animal. And it's a safe and tasty way to introduce walnuts to babies. This puree is a great way to add protein, zinc, and vitamin E to your baby's diet. A 4-tablespoon serving supplies a third of your baby's daily protein, a quarter of his vitamin E, and one-fifth of his zinc. This puree is also great as a spread on crackers and toast.

MAKES 1 CUP (4 SERVINGS)

1 tablespoon neutral-flavored oil, such as safflower, sunflower, or grapeseed

1½ cups chopped onions

2 cups chopped mushrooms of choice

⅓ cup chopped walnuts

5 tablespoons unsweetened soy milk or other nondairy milk

¼ cup Apple Puree (page 59) or unsweetened applesauce

In a large skillet, heat the oil over medium heat. Add the onions and cook, stirring occasionally, until they start to become translucent, about 5 minutes. Add the mushrooms and cook, stirring occasionally, until tender, about 5 minutes. Add the walnuts and cook, stirring occasionally, for 5 minutes or so more. Do not let the mixture burn; you may need to add a little more oil and turn down the heat a bit. Remove from the heat and let cool. Transfer the mixture to a blender or food processor and add the soy milk and apple puree. Blend until smooth. Add more soy milk as needed until you reach the desired consistency. Portion ¼ cup of the pâté puree into a small bowl to serve now and store the remainder in an airtight container in the refrigerator for up to 3 days.

Variation For more advanced eaters, omit the apple puree, add a pinch of freshly ground black pepper, and season with salt to taste.

PLAY WITH
YOUR FOOD

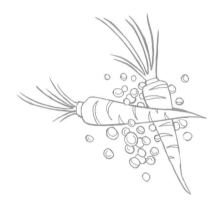

SMASHED WHITE BEANS WITH ONION AND HERBS

CASHEW CREAMED KALE

BABY GUACABOWLIE

WHAT-HAVE-YOU CHICKPEA MILLET STEW

CAULI QUINOA CASSEROLE

BABY MAC-O'-LANTERN AND CHEEZE

DAHLIA'S BABY DAL

KHICHDI

Babies feel so empowered when they get to feed themselves. Their instinct is to put everything in their mouths anyway, so when it's actually edible—oh boy! In this chapter, we introduce foods with a bit of texture that babies will enjoy raking with their hands and putting into their mouths . . . and onto their cheeks, noses, foreheads, and bellies! It is all to be encouraged, since sensory play is important for their development and gives them an extra level of familiarity with new foods.

We also go full-on with flavor in these recipes. We don't include any salt, but there's no skimping on seasonings. We introduce babies to eighteen different herbs and spices and several fresh allium vegetables, from red onions to leeks. If a recipe calls for a specific herb or allium that you don't have at that particular moment, feel free to swap it out for something similar or something else you like. The point is to have fun introducing baby to new flavors, which will serve you both well in the future.

SMASHED WHITE BEANS WITH ONION AND HERBS

Now is the time to get them used to having "stuff" in their food! Those green flecks aren't just garnish—they're a good source of antioxidants. We use navy beans, but you can use another white bean instead. We also adore the French flavor that a little bit of herbes de Provence lends to the dish. To turn it into a full meal, add ¼ cup Carrot Puree (page 59) or Butternut Squash Puree (page 61), either on the side or mixed in.

A 3-tablespoon serving of Smashed White Beans provides lots of protein, as well as around 15 percent of the iron and calcium and more than 20 percent of the zinc a growing baby needs each day.

MAKES 1 CUP (ABOUT 5 SERVINGS)

1 tablespoon neutral-flavored oil, such as safflower, sunflower, or grapeseed

¼ cup grated onion

1 (15-ounce) can navy beans or other white beans, drained and rinsed

2 to 3 teaspoons finely chopped fresh parsley

⅛ teaspoon herbes de Provence, or more to taste (optional; see Note)

In a large skillet, heat the oil over low heat. Add the onion and cook, stirring, until soft, 2 to 3 minutes. Add the beans and cook, stirring occasionally, until the beans are heated through, a few minutes more. Add the parsley and herbes de Provence (if using) and stir. Remove from the heat and mash with a fork either a little or a lot, depending on your baby's comfort level with chewing food. Let cool for a few minutes, then serve.

> Note You can make your own herbes de Provence blend using 2 parts dried savory, thyme, and basil to 1 part dried rosemary, tarragon, and, if you have it, culinary lavender.

CASHEW CREAMED KALE

When Marisa was filming *Vegucated*, Dr. Joel Fuhrman brought her and the three soon-to-be vegans-for-six-weeks featured in the documentary to his house and let them taste some of the healthy foods his family eats, including his son's favorite food, cashew creamed kale. When Marisa's daughter, Emmeline, was a baby, Marisa mixed the Cashew Chive Spread from Dreena Burton's cookbook, *Let Them Eat Vegan*, with steamed kale, and it quickly became beloved by both Marisa and Emmeline.

Four tablespoons of this creamy spread give your baby's bones a boost, supplying more than 15 percent of the needed calcium in a well-absorbed form, thanks to the kale. This dish is also an easy way to add protein, zinc, potassium, and vitamin C.

MAKES 1 CUP (4 SERVINGS)

3 cups packed roughly chopped stemmed kale leaves

⅓ cup Cashew Chive Spread (page 196), prepared without salt

Fill a medium pot with about 1 inch of water and place a steamer basket in the pot. Cover the pot and bring the water to a simmer over medium-high heat. Place the kale in the basket and steam for 10 to 12 minutes (this is a good time to make the Cashew Chive Spread, if you haven't already). Remove the kale from the heat and let cool, then drain it in a colander and press out any excess water with your hands.

Finely chop the kale and transfer it to a medium bowl. Add the Cashew Chive Spread and stir to combine evenly. Serve immediately. Store any leftovers in an airtight container in the fridge for up to 1 day.

BABY GUACABOWLIE

A balanced meal in one little bowl. For a simpler version, you can use plain mashed avocado and plain beans, but this bowl has more flavor and protein. A baby serving (about a third of the recipe, or ¼ cup) delivers around 20 percent of a baby's daily protein, along with 10 percent of your baby's recommended daily zinc and a nice amount of B vitamins.

MAKES ¾ CUP (ABOUT 3 SERVINGS)

¼ cup Avocado for Your Sweet Pea (page 68)

¼ cup Cauliflower Rice (page 156)

¼ cup Magic Beans (page 167) or plain beans, mashed

1 teaspoon chopped fresh cilantro, for garnish (optional)

Place all of the ingredients into a baby-size bowl and serve.

WHAT-HAVE-YOU CHICKPEA MILLET STEW

This was a staple in Marisa's home when her youngest was a baby. It really fits the bill when you want an all-in-one dish that you can throw together with whatever you have on hand in the fridge or freezer.

Just 4 tablespoons of this stew deliver generous amounts of many nutrients that support your baby's growth and development, including 40 percent of the recommended daily folate, 20 percent of the vitamin A and protein, and 16 percent of the zinc.

MAKES 1 CUP (4 SERVINGS)

1 teaspoon neutral-flavored oil, such as safflower, sunflower, or grapeseed oil

Heaping 1 tablespoon grated or finely chopped onion

¼ teaspoon dried savory or your favorite dried herb

⅓ cup water or no-salt-added vegetable broth

½ cup cooked millet

¼ cup Bean Puree (page 61), prepared with chickpeas, or mashed chickpeas

3 tablespoons Carrot Puree (page 59), Butternut Squash Puree (page 61), or Sweet Potato Puree (page 61)

3 tablespoons Apple Puree (page 59) or Pear Puree (page 59)

⅛ teaspoon salt (optional; only for older kids and adults, not babies)

In a small pot, heat the oil over medium-low heat for a minute or two. Add the onion and savory to the pot and cook, stirring occasionally, until the onion starts to become translucent, 2 to 3 minutes.

Add the water and cook for 2 to 3 minutes more. Add the millet and the bean, vegetable, and fruit purees to the pot and stir until well combined or until frozen purees are thawed and well combined. Remove from the heat and let cool, then spoon out baby's portion and store the rest in an airtight container for up to 3 days or if serving to older kids, spoon out their portion, add salt, and stir.

Note If you have frozen chickpea, vegetable, or apple puree on hand, there's no need to defrost or reheat it before adding it to the pan in this recipe. Just be sure to stir until the frozen puree is thawed.

CAULI QUINOA CASSEROLE

Marisa's kids loved this simple dish as babies and do so even now as "big kids." In each 6-tablespoon serving, this powerhouse of a recipe delivers 15 percent of the iron, 40 percent of the zinc, and almost half the protein your baby needs daily. It also supplies an impressive amount of magnesium, potassium, and folate.

MAKES 4 CUPS (ABOUT 10 SERVINGS)

About 2 cups cauliflower florets (from about ½ head cauliflower)

1 small leek, white and light green parts sliced and rinsed very well to remove grit (a generous ½ cup), ¼ cup chopped onion, or 1 teaspoon onion powder

1 (15-ounce) can adzuki beans or other canned beans, drained and rinsed

Scant ½ teaspoon salt (optional; only for older kids and adults, not babies)

3 cups cooked quinoa, cooked in no-salt-added vegetable broth or water

¾ cup shredded vegan cheese (optional)

Preheat the oven to 375°F.

Fill a medium saucepan with about 1 inch of water and place a steamer basket in the pot. Cover the pot and bring the water to a simmer over high heat, then adjust the heat to a steady simmer. Put the cauliflower and leeks in the basket, cover, and steam until they can be pierced easily with a fork, 10 to 12 minutes. Transfer the cauliflower and leeks to a blender or food processor. Add the beans and salt (if using) and process until smooth. Transfer the cauliflower-bean mixture to a 9-inch square baking dish (or rectangular equivalent), add the quinoa, and stir together until well combined. Spread the mixture evenly in the baking dish. Sprinkle the cheese (if using) evenly over the top. Bake until the cheese has melted, about 20 minutes. You might need to switch the oven to broil for the last 5 minutes to melt it fully. Remove from the oven and let cool, then serve.

Store any leftovers in small freezer-safe containers in the freezer for up to 3 months, and thaw them whenever you need easy meals in the future.

BABY MAC-O'-LANTERN AND CHEEZE

Pumpkin takes center stage in this baby take on mac 'n' cheese. A ¼-cup serving of Baby Mac-o'-Lantern and Cheeze supplies about a third of an eight-month-old's daily protein, close to 40 percent of the vitamin A they need, and plenty of B vitamins. If you use a brand of nutritional yeast that contains vitamin B$_{12}$, this recipe will help to meet your baby's needs for this essential nutrient.

1 tablespoon vegan butter, such as Earth Balance

1 cup canned or homemade pumpkin puree

1 teaspoon apple cider vinegar

½ teaspoon garlic powder

1¼ cups no-salt-added vegetable broth

½ cup nutritional yeast

¾ cup dried orzo

Sea salt (optional; only for older kids and adults, not babies)

In a small to medium saucepan, melt the vegan butter with the pumpkin puree over medium-low heat. Stir in the vinegar and garlic powder until fully incorporated. Carefully pour in the broth and stir or whisk to fully combine with the pumpkin mixture. Stir in the nutritional yeast. Add the orzo and stir to evenly distribute it. Cook until the mixture starts to bubble, then reduce the heat to low and cook, stirring every few minutes so the orzo does not stick to the bottom as it cooks, until the orzo has absorbed the liquid and the dish has a nice risottolike consistency, about 30 minutes. Serve and enjoy! Store leftovers in an airtight container in the fridge for a day or two or in the freezer for up to 3 months.

Variation For bigger kids and adults, our Vegan Parm Sprinkle (page 186) is a great topping to this recipe.

DAHLIA'S BABY DAL

Think 10-20-30. That's about how much iron (10 percent of a six-to-twelve-month-old's recommended daily intake), zinc (20 percent), and protein (30 percent) a 3-tablespoon serving of Dahlia's Baby Dal delivers.

by Leinana Two Moons

MAKES 2 TO 2½ CUPS (10 TO 13 SERVINGS)

1 teaspoon olive oil

1 cup dried red lentils

½ teaspoon mild yellow curry powder

In a small pot, heat the oil over medium heat. Add the red lentils and cook, stirring to coat with the oil, about 30 seconds. Add the curry powder and stir again for 30 seconds to coat.

Add 3 cups water, then raise the heat to high and bring to a boil. Reduce the heat to low and simmer, stirring occasionally to prevent anything sticking to the bottom, until the dal is thick and the lentils are tender, about 20 minutes. We like a thick consistency, but if you prefer it a bit soupier, or if it becomes too thick before it has finished cooking, simply add more water ½ cup at a time until it reaches your desired consistency.

Variation For more advanced eaters (this is how Dahlia likes it now): Add ½ teaspoon dried ginger and ½ teaspoon ground cumin along with the curry powder and stir 1 teaspoon vegetable bouillon (we like Better Than Bouillon Organic Vegetable Base) into the 3 cups water before adding it to the pot. When the dal is finished, season it with salt and freshly ground black pepper to taste.

"My daughter Dahlia is a super-picky eater. Like, a super-picky eater. But ever since she was a baby, she would eat this dal, and at five years old, it's still one of her favorite meals. Over time, we've added spices and other additions, making it more and more interesting. But it's still, at heart, a very simple comfort dish. You can start with our mildest version for babies and toddlers, and eventually make it spicier as they grow more adventurous."

—Leinana

KHICHDI

Khichdi is a great way to add protein to your baby's diet. Just 4 balls (about 4 tablespoons) have around 20 percent of the protein an older baby needs each day. That same amount provides more than 10 percent of the daily recommended amount of thiamine, niacin, and vitamin B_6 for an older baby.

by Christina and Pulin Modi

MAKES 3½ CUPS OR ABOUT 56 TABLESPOON-SIZE BALLS (14 SERVINGS)

2 tablespoons olive oil

1 medium red onion, diced

1 cup diced tomatoes (canned or fresh)

1 teaspoon ground turmeric

1 teaspoon ground cumin

1 teaspoon ground coriander

1 teaspoon salt (optional; only for older kids and adults, not babies)

½ cup uncooked brown rice

½ cup moong dal (dried split yellow lentils)

In a medium saucepan, heat the oil over medium heat. Add the onion, tomatoes, turmeric, cumin, coriander, and salt (if using) and cook, stirring, until the onion is translucent.

Rinse the brown rice and moong dal in a fine-mesh sieve and drain, then add them to the pan. Add water—use 2½ cups for a thicker consistency (which will be easier to form into balls) or 3½ cups for a thinner consistency. Bring the water to a boil, then reduce the heat to low/medium. Cover and simmer until rice and dal are soft, about 40 minutes.

The khichdi may not look like it will hold together in a ball, but it will! To form balls, let the khichdi cool, then refrigerate it for a couple of hours; it will thicken as it cools. Scoop roughly 1-tablespoon portions of khichdi with your hands and roll into balls. The khichdi balls can be eaten cold or microwaved for 30 to 45 seconds to serve warm. Alternatively, you can just serve khichdi in a bowl without rolling it into balls. Leftovers can be stored in an airtight container in the fridge for up to 3 days or in the freezer for up to 3 months.

———————

"Khichdi is a comfort food common throughout India and is a popular dish for babies and toddlers. It's healthy and tasty and easy to eat when you're sick or you just want something relatively simple. Peas, carrots, potatoes, and other veggies can be added instead of, or in addition to, the tomato and onion. Khichdi can be served in a bowl as is or can be rolled into balls. Our son, Satya, loves eating this in any form, including balls, which is less messy for him to eat."

—Christina and Pulin

GOOD GRUB
TO GRAB

AVOCADO TOAST FINGERS WITH NOOCH

TOFU SCRAMBLE

TOP O' THE MORNING GREEN POWER PANCAKES

CHICKPEA–SWEET POTATO CROQUETTES

SOUTHWESTERN BABY BOWL

SWEET POTATO WEDGES

GREEN BEANS AND ALMOND CREAM

TEETHING RUSKS

At around nine to ten months, a baby will typically have the fine motor development to use a pincer grasp, which is coordinating the index finger and thumb to pick up and hold a small item like a pea. It's a big milestone! Before that, they can grab something with their fist—a sweet potato stick, some quinoa, your hair. The recipes in this chapter are for foods that allow babies to take advantage of both grasps to feed themselves. Parents might even recognize these foods as something they would like to eat, too!

AVOCADO TOAST FINGERS WITH NOOCH

Three kid-friendly vegan staples together in perfect harmony: toast, avocado, and nooch. And all three of these staples combine to supply all the thiamine, riboflavin, vitamin B_6, and vitamin B_{12} your baby needs in a day in a ½-slice serving. That same serving size also delivers a hearty helping of zinc, vitamin E, and potassium. Be sure your nooch has vitamin B_{12}; not all brands do.

MAKES 4 (2 SERVINGS)

1 slice whole-grain bread
¼ small avocado, mashed
1 teaspoon nutritional yeast

Lightly toast the bread. Spread the avocado on it. Sprinkle with nutritional yeast. Cut into 4 long sticks.

TOFU SCRAMBLE

The seasonings in this recipe were inspired by the Southern Fried Tofu recipe in *Vegan Vittles* by Joanne Stepaniak. A 3-tablespoon serving of Tofu Scramble has more than 40 percent of the protein and 10 percent of the zinc an older baby needs daily. If you make it with vitamin B_{12}—fortified nutritional yeast and calcium-set tofu, a serving will go a long way toward meeting your baby's daily needs for calcium and vitamin B_{12}.

MAKES 2 CUPS (ABOUT 10 SERVINGS)

1 (14-ounce) block firm or extra-firm tofu

⅔ cup nutritional yeast

½ teaspoon garlic powder

½ teaspoon onion powder

¼ teaspoon paprika

Rounded ¼ teaspoon salt (optional; only for older kids and adults, not babies)

⅛ teaspoon dried dill

⅛ teaspoon dried basil

⅛ teaspoon dried oregano (see Note)

⅛ teaspoon mild curry powder

⅛ teaspoon mustard powder

1 tablespoon neutral-flavored oil, such as safflower, sunflower or grapeseed

Drain the tofu. If you have a tofu press, follow the manufacturer's instructions to press excess liquid from the tofu. If you don't have a press, wrap the block of tofu in a kitchen towel, place it on a plate, and set another plate on top. Stack a couple of heavy cookbooks on the plate and let it stand for 15 to 20 minutes. Gravity will press some of the liquid out.

Meanwhile, in a medium to large bowl, stir together the nutritional yeast, garlic powder, onion powder, paprika, salt (if using), dill, basil, oregano, curry, and mustard until well combined.

In a large skillet, heat the oil over medium-high heat. Unwrap the tofu and use your hands to crumble it into the bowl with the seasonings (kids might enjoy helping with this part). Mix with your hands until well incorporated. Transfer the tofu mixture to the pan and cook, stirring occasionally, until the tofu has firmed up and is golden brown, 12 to 15 minutes. Let the scramble cool for a few minutes, then serve.

Note Oregano is an antigalactagogue, which means it hinders lactation, so if you're breastfeeding and will be sharing this scramble with your baby, omit it.

Variation Add-ins for more advanced palates: Sauté ½ cup finely chopped onion in the oil for 5 minutes before adding the tofu. You can also add ⅓ cup chopped tomatoes, bell peppers, or mushrooms, or a mix of these—whatever you like!

TOP O' THE MORNING GREEN POWER PANCAKES

Why should we wait for Saint Patrick's Day to sneak spinach into a breakfast favorite like pancakes? These certainly are "green power pancakes." Four mini pancakes, made with calcium- and vitamin B_{12}–fortified nondairy milk, deliver more than half your baby's recommended daily calcium and vitamin B_{12}. Add in 25 percent of iron needs and 30 percent of zinc needs, and these are some super green power pancakes!

MAKES 24 SILVER DOLLAR PANCAKES (6 SERVINGS)

1 cup nondairy milk

¾ cup packed spinach

¼ teaspoon pure vanilla extract

⅔ cup whole-wheat pastry flour

5 tablespoons iron-fortified baby cereal (see Note)

1 tablespoon chia seeds

2 teaspoons baking powder

½ teaspoon ground cinnamon

¼ teaspoon salt (only for older kids and adults, not babies)

Coconut oil spray or melted coconut oil, for greasing

Berry Chia Jam (page 198) or sliced strawberries (optional, for topping)

In a blender, combine the milk, spinach, and vanilla and blend on high until the mixture turns green. In a large bowl, combine the pastry flour, baby cereal, chia seeds, baking powder, cinnamon, and salt (if using). Add the milk mixture and mix until combined.

Preheat the oven to 200°F.

As the batter sets and the chia seeds soak up the liquid, warm a large skillet or griddle over medium-low heat. Once the skillet or griddle is hot (but not screaming hot), spray or drizzle the surface with coconut oil. Scoop single tablespoons of the batter onto the hot surface and cook until the edges of the pancakes are dry, 3 to 4 minutes, then flip and cook until the underside is golden brown, another minute or two. Transfer the pancakes to an oven-safe serving dish or baking pan and keep them warm in the oven while you cook the remaining batter.

Serve the pancakes warm, topped with chia jam or sliced strawberries, if desired. (The vitamin C in strawberries helps unlock the iron power!)

Note You can substitute ½ cup of rolled oats for the baby cereal, but it won't have as much iron.

CHICKPEA–SWEET POTATO CROQUETTES

This recipe makes a lot of yummy croquettes! It's a great food to stash away in the freezer for future meals. There's so much goodness in such a small package! Four croquettes deliver 25 percent of the zinc and vitamin A and more than 20 percent of the calcium and iron that a six-to-twelve-month-old needs daily.

MAKES ABOUT 36 (9 SERVINGS)

1 bay leaf (optional)

1 sweet potato, peeled and coarsely chopped

1 tomato, chopped

½ cup finely chopped shallots

¼ cup fortified baby cereal (any kind)

1 teaspoon dried basil

¾ teaspoon garlic powder

½ teaspoon paprika

¼ teaspoon salt (optional; only for older kids and adults, not babies)

Pinch of ground cinnamon

1 (15-ounce) can chickpeas, drained and rinsed

Bread crumbs or cornmeal, for coating

Preheat the oven to 400°F. Grease two baking sheets with cooking spray or oil of choice or line them with parchment paper.

Fill a medium pot with 1 inch of water and add the bay leaf to the water, if desired. Place a steamer basket in the pot, cover, and bring the water to a simmer over high heat. Put the potato, tomato, and shallots in the basket, cover, and steam until fork-tender, 15 to 20 minutes, stirring once after 10 minutes. Uncover the pot and let the vegetables cool a little, then transfer them to a large bowl.

Add the baby cereal, basil, garlic powder, paprika, salt (if using), and cinnamon to the bowl with the veggies and mash with a potato masher until well incorporated. Add the chickpeas and mash again, but not so much that the chickpeas turn to total mush; you want to retain a nice texture and some chunks.

Pour some bread crumbs into a shallow bowl. Using a teaspoon, scoop out portions of the mash and form them into balls with your hands, setting them on a large plate as you go. Roll the balls in the bread crumbs to coat completely, setting the coated croquettes on the prepared baking sheets. Flatten each one gently with your palm or a spatula. If you like, you can spray the tops with oil to help them turn golden as they bake. Bake for 25 to 30 minutes. Remove from the oven, let cool, and serve! Store leftovers in an airtight container in the fridge for up to 3 days or in the freezer for up to a month.

SOUTHWESTERN BABY BOWL

The Nacho Cashew Cheese Sauce is what really makes this dish sparkle and come together in a super-yummy way. A baby serving is a bowlful of nutrition, with more than 30 percent of the protein, 25 percent of the zinc, and 10 percent of the iron an older baby needs daily. The tomatoes add a significant amount of vitamin C, which promotes iron absorption.

MAKES ABOUT ⅓ CUP (1 SERVING)

2 tablespoons canned pinto beans, drained and rinsed

2 tablespoons cooked quinoa

2 tablespoons chopped (small, bite-size pieces) fresh tomato

1 tablespoon Nacho Cashew Cheese Sauce (page 195), prepared without salt

Place the beans, quinoa, and tomato in a kid's bowl. Drizzle the cheese sauce on top and serve.

SWEET POTATO WEDGES

Oh, those wonderful sweet potatoes! Just 2 sticks supply almost half the vitamin A an older baby needs in a day, along with more than 10 percent of the potassium needed.

by Lisa Pitman

MAKES 8 WEDGES (4 SERVINGS)

1 medium sweet potato, cut lengthwise into 8 wedges

1 to 2 teaspoons olive oil or melted coconut oil

Preheat the oven to 400°F. Line a baking sheet with parchment paper.

Put the sweet potato in a large bowl, drizzle with the oil, and toss until well coated. Spread the wedges on the prepared baking sheet. Bake until soft all the way through, about 25 minutes, flipping the wedges once halfway. Let cool almost to room temperature before serving.

Note Leaving the peel on gives the wedges more structure, which helps little hands pick them up. Crinkle cutters for french fries also work well to make easy-to-pick-up sweet potato sticks.

"Many babies love the smooth texture of sweet potatoes as one of their first foods. Parents love that this superfood is a powerhouse of nutrition. With my daughter Isla, a determined little soul, we went the finger-food route rather than starting with purees. She loved being in charge of her meal, and we were amazed by how she was able to get the flesh away from the peel of the sweet potato on her first attempt."

—Lisa

GREEN BEANS AND ALMOND CREAM

Tender green beans are a perfect finger food for eager hands, and coating the beans with almond cream boosts the flavor and nutrition. A 6-tablespoon serving of this recipe supplies a quarter of the antioxidant vitamin E that an older infant needs each day, along with more than 10 percent of the recommended daily protein and potassium.

12 ounces green beans, cut in half or into thirds (about 3½ cups)

½ cup raw almonds

¼ cup no-salt-added vegetable broth

¼ cup unsweetened almond milk or other nondairy milk

1 teaspoon fresh lemon juice

½ teaspoon onion powder

½ garlic clove, minced

Place the beans in a large saucepan and add enough water to cover them. Bring the water to a boil over high heat, then reduce the heat to maintain a simmer and cook the beans until tender, 10 to 12 minutes. Drain.

Meanwhile, in a blender, combine the almonds, broth, milk, lemon juice, onion powder, and garlic and blend on high until creamy and smooth.

Add ½ cup of the almond cream to the beans and toss or stir until they are well coated, then serve. (You'll have some almond cream left over; store it in an airtight container in the fridge for up to 3 days. It tastes great on toast with avocado and tomato.)

Note If you're not using a Vitamix or other high-powered blender, soak the almonds in water for 2 hours, then drain.

TEETHING RUSKS

See note for a variation that simplifies this recipe even more. These are very mildly flavored; most of the flavor of the fruit or veggie puree that you put in it will likely bake out of it. You can add a pinch of cinnamon or pumpkin pie spice to the batter or sprinkle cinnamon or ground freeze-dried berries on the rusks after baking. Get creative, depending on the age of your child and what you have available. As with all foods, be sure to supervise baby while she is gnawing on these to prevent choking.

One smaller rusk adds some protein to an older baby's diet, along with about 10 percent of the daily magnesium and thiamine that a six-to-eight-month-old needs.

by Jenna Matheson

MAKES 9 LARGE OR 12 SMALL

2 tablespoons whole flaxseeds

1½ cups spelt flour or oat flour

½ teaspoon baking powder

½ cup fruit or vegetable puree (such as apple, pear, banana, pumpkin, sweet potato, broccoli, or green peas)

Ground cinnamon or ground freeze-dried strawberries or blueberries, for sprinkling (optional)

Preheat the oven to 350°F.

In a small saucepan, combine the flaxseeds and ½ cup water. Bring to a boil over high heat, then reduce the heat to low and simmer, stirring continuously, until the mixture becomes gloopy, thick, and gel-like, about 3 minutes. Pour the flaxseed mixture through a fine-mesh sieve into a small bowl and discard the seeds (you may need to stir the mixture with a spoon to encourage the gel to come through the sieve). You should have about 3 tablespoons of clear gel. If the gel isn't coming through, return the mixture to the pot, add a few tablespoons more water, stir, and try again.

Add the flour, baking powder, and fruit or vegetable puree to a food processor with the flax gel. Combine the ingredients and knead together into a ball of dough.

Divide the dough evenly into 9 pieces (for larger rusks) or 12 pieces (for smaller ones) and press them into silicone molds, or shape the pieces with your hands and put them on a baking sheet lined with parchment paper.

Continued

Sprinkle the rusks with cinnamon or ground freeze-dried berries, if desired. Bake for 25 to 40 minutes, depending on how firm you want them to be. Let cool, then remove from the molds or the baking sheet and store in an airtight container at room temperature for up to 2 weeks.

Variation Instead of making the flax gel, stir together 3 tablespoons flax meal and 1 tablespoon warm water in a small bowl, then let the mixture thicken for a few minutes. Meanwhile, combine the other ingredients in a medium bowl, then add the flax meal mixture. Combine and knead together into a ball of dough. The resulting rusks will be slightly softer, meaning babies can bite off pieces more easily and extra caution should be given due to choking concerns.

"When my children went through teething, it was no joke. I did frozen fruit sticks, frozen wet washcloths, and teething toys galore, but what my kids loved the best were my four-ingredient teething rusks. I could whip these up with ingredients I already had in the fridge or pantry, and they lasted two weeks in an airtight container—that is, if they weren't all eaten right away! They are a firm biscuit that dissolves in the baby's mouth as she chews, chews, and chews some more!

"I use a rectangular silicone bar mold or a donut mold to form them easily into a kid-friendly shape, or you can just shape them into little sticks, twists, knots, or logs with your hands. I've also braided three pieces of dough together, which lends a bit of texture. One batch makes enough dough that you can make several shapes per batch, and when your child is irritable and starts to assert his/her independence, giving him or her three different shapes to choose from is a win."

—Jenna

Part Two

TODDLERS
+ BEYOND

Congrats! You have a toddler! A whole world of culinary delights awaits your child.

Also, our condolences. You have a toddler, and you have to face the challenges that come with feeding a growing person with a growing sense of independence. Where once was a beautiful baby who happily consumed all manner of delicious, nutritious foods, there now might be a child who refuses to eat, pooh-poohs his old favorites, and may not be interested in eating much at all. It may leave parents wondering, "Who is this imposter and can she run on two tablespoons of breakfast a day?" This phase can be more fraught for plant-powered parents, who may question if their little one is getting the nutrition he needs. Many of the foods that nonvegan littles eat exclusively are off-limits to vegan toddlers. We say, congrats! You have a vegan toddler with so many vitamin-rich staples in her diet that you likely never even tried when you were a toddler.

Our nutritionist, Reed Mangels, does a wonderful job of addressing picky eating (see page 23). She explains what it may mean, how toddlers' slowed rate of growth affects their appetites, what's developmentally appropriate for their age, and ways to get your child to accept a variety of foods.

If you have found yourself begging, bribing, and even dancing for your kiddo to take "just one bite" of this or that, we've been there, we feel you, and we have a few thoughts and ideas of our own.

Perhaps most important, you might find it comforting to know that a toddler's initial wariness toward leafy greens might have little to do with your parenting or their willfulness. It may at least be partly an evolutionary survival instinct. In *The No-Cry Picky Eater Solution*, Elizabeth Pantley writes about how breast milk and fruits that are safe to eat are sweet. "Poisonous plants, toxic chemicals, and spoiled foods, however, are sour or bitter, so a child's natural instinct is to avoid anything with those types of flavors."

Genetics are also partly at play. Pantley points out, "Some studies show that if you disliked broccoli, fish, or fuzzy food (such as peaches and kiwis) when you were younger, then chances are your child will dislike the same sorts of foods, since certain likes and dislikes may be part of her makeup." Marisa took a DNA test that showed that she had a genetically predisposed heightened sensitivity to bitter tastes. Her husband, David, ate nary a vegetable as a child. Their children seem to be doomed to dislike bitter veggies, and for now their son, Gabriel, actively dislikes them. Yet both parents now crave brussels sprouts and kale, so they know it can be overcome.

Bee Wilson, author of *First Bite*, a highly recommended book for parents looking to expand their children's palates, claims, "Overall, the evidence for tastes being heritable is very modest, accounting for only around 20 percent—at most—of the variation in foods eaten." Wilson points to studies that show that exposure determines what children prefer, and the environment in which they learn to eat is perhaps the most significant factor of all. According to Wilson's research, a stronger predictor in forming tastes is access to healthy food.

Study after study shows that parents who eat more vegetables have children who eat more vegetables and grow up to eat more vegetables. If children are served veggies at every meal growing up, they develop not only a familiarity with them but also a sense that a meal is not complete without veggies, and will likely be more inclined to include them.

Teaching by example is perhaps the most powerful tool of all. When we checked out *Black Mama Vegan*, Aimbriel Lasley's social media account, and saw the super-healthy dishes her kids were eating, we asked her to send in a recipe (see page 160) and wanted to know all her magical ways for getting her kids to love good stuff. She says, "When we transitioned to being vegan, this lifestyle change meant I was cooking more often at home while also introducing new foods. My kitchen is also where a lot of conversations and family time happen. Quite naturally as I began trying new things, my boys became curious. One of my boys noticed me using pumpkin seeds in my smoothies, oatmeal, etc. He asked to taste them plain (unsalted). Although he didn't care for them plain, he decided to incorporate them in his oatmeal, too, along with raisins, cinnamon, and hemp! I talked to him about the nutrients and how they could help his body grow. We now eat them with a dash of oil, nutritional yeast, and salt—yum! Exposure is everything, and I'm grateful for this lifestyle and its impact on our family."

Bee Wilson writes, "If liking is a consequence of familiarity, it follows that children are bound to like a narrower range of foods at first than adults, because they haven't tried as many. Problems arise when parents interpret this temporary wariness as something permanent. This is an easy mistake to make. The key period for acquiring preferences is toddlerdom, from ages one to three. But this coincides with the time in children's lives when they are most maddeningly, willfully reluctant to try anything new." To some extent, this is a waiting game. According to Wilson, "This stage reaches a peak between the ages of two and six," so parents of one-year-olds only have about five more years to go—hang in there, guys! (Sigh.)

HOW TO GET KIDS TO TRY NEW FOODS

1. Start out small.

Nutritionist Reed Mangels recommends starting out with small quantities. We started putting shards of healthy veggies on our kids' plates to encourage acceptance and familiarity. Over time they began to eat whole chunks of yellow pepper or tomato and slices of cucumber.

2. Pair it with a food they already like.

Kate Samela, author of *Give Peas a Chance*, introduces readers to "the safety food," which is "one food that you are certain your toddler will accept." She explains, "The safety food serves to disarm that immediate protest or reaction of panic when the toddler finds new food on his plate. Your toddler might have fewer objections once his eye catches the safety food."

3. Presentation, presentation, presentation!

There are all manner of novel ways to present new foods. Making faces or animal shapes out of foods seems laborious, but it does spark interest. Using cookie cutters can turn foods into fun shapes. What seems tedious and time-consuming to a parent might just delight the child enough to try something new.

4. Incentivize!

Some call it bribery; we prefer to call it incentivizing. Keith E. Williams, PhD, BCBA, the director of the Penn State Children's Hospital Feeding Program and expert in behavioral treatment of feeding disorders in children says, "Persons, whether an infant or adult, learn preferences through repeated tasting, in the amount as small as a grain of rice. The key is repeated tasting, with most children requiring tastes on ten or more occasions. Neither looking at the food, sniffing the food, licking the food, nor playing with the food seems to help; the research shows ingestion is the key. While repeated tasting is necessary, numerous methods have been used to encourage tasting." What kinds of methods, you might ask? He clarifies, "Incentives, in the form of access to preferred activities or objects, is one method that multiple researchers have demonstrated to be successful."

What might this look like? Marisa's good friend Annie Shannon, author of *Betty Goes Vegan* and *Mastering the Art of Vegan Cooking*, describes how she got her five-year-old to try new foods: "Our daughter was never a picky eater. She loved trying new baby foods and would try a bite of anything I was eating until one day she took a great big bite of a plum so sour it made her shiver and cry. After that she started sticking to a small and fairly bland selection of food. When she asked for a real Barbie in an astronaut suit, we started the new foods sticker chart about ten minutes later. Fifteen stickers and new foods later and she got her $7 doll."

The Fred & Friends Dinner Winner tray has a built-in incentive. This plate resembles a board game, with nine spaces on the board where you can put various small portions of food, the last one being the special surprise "treat" that you get once you've tried all the foods that preceded it. Marisa's kids took to this tray like wildfire, and it was a surefire way to get her kids to try every food on the tray throughout their toddler years.

5. Offer variety.

One major appeal of the Dinner Winner tray is that there are so many spaces for a variety of foods. There's a reason why buffets, tapas, dim sum, and thalis are beloved around the world. Children love variety and options during mealtime. Even using muffin tins is a good way to create your own trays for a similar lots-of-little-dishes effect.

6. Boost flavor.

Yes, it's so important to get children to appreciate the natural flavors of foods without a lot of added salt, sugar, or fat, and if your kid loves steamed asparagus, you win parenting! If you are a mere mortal like the rest of us and your toddler won't even look at a stalk of asparagus, try sprinkling it with lemon juice, garlic powder, oil, salt, or nutritional yeast before baking it. That made all the difference for Marisa's daughter. Now she likes asparagus.

You will see a lot of nutritional yeast ("nooch") in our recipes, and for good reason. Not only does it provide important vitamins for plant-strong kids, but it's a go-to ingredient that makes anything yummy and kid-friendly without added salt (see page 7).

7. The blender is your friend.

For some reason, many toddlers freak out if there is "stuff" in their food. If there are—God forbid—discernible onions in a dish and the kids refuse to even taste it, it goes in the blender or food processor. The healthy "stuff" is in there, but they can't see it. We have blended soups, sauces, and even the beans in quesadillas, burritos, and tacos to "hide" the good stuff. Yes, the kids need to be exposed to and get used to "stuff," so we continue to expose them, but blending never fails at our house.

8. Teach them about plant superpowers.

Plant foods are superfoods, and little kids love to know what superpowers plants can give them. You might remember being told by adults that carrots helped you see really well. We've pulled that out on several occasions. We also share which foods make them super smart (like blueberries) and give kids "big muscles" (see Muscly Marinara, page 192)—the kids flex their muscles after every bite.

9. Get your child involved.

From vegan dad Steve Kain:

"We have found that asking our daughter to take part in the cooking process is a great way to expose her to a variety of foods and also encourages positive discussion around food. We identify kid-friendly tasks like stirring, garnishing, and setting the table that she is able to complete on her own. She is visibly proud to be a helper and this pride translates to the table when it's time to eat. She is so excited to discuss, taste, and share her cooking accomplishments with her family."

10. Pressuring can have the opposite effect.

First Bite author Bee Wilson adds a critical component to the advice to expose toddlers to food repeatedly: it should be positive. "If a food is repeatedly tasted under conditions of coercion or stress," she says, "the exposure may have the effect of reinforcing rather than reversing an aversion." She cites a 2006 study by Leann Birch and colleagues in which young children were either pressured or not pressured to finish their soup. According to the study's abstract, "Children consumed significantly more food when they were not pressured to eat, and they made overwhelmingly fewer negative comments."

11. Make it fun.

Vegan dad Steve Kain has some great ideas for increasing enjoyment at the table when dealing with a picky eater like his five-year-old daughter, Evelyn:

"We have found that introducing something different or special to mealtime can shift the focus away from the food itself and actually encourages your child to eat more. For example, we light candles on our dining room table for almost every dinner. Our daughter loves to help dim the lights and watch as I light the candles. During dinner, we go around the table and talk about our day with each of us sharing 'one rose and one thorn.' Another example is having a family picnic. This doesn't need to be a huge, scheduled ordeal. Sometimes it can be as simple as spreading a blanket on the living room floor and using a small table or tray."

We love Steve's "Cooking Competition" game idea, which also makes mealtimes fun and increases his daughter's chance of trying something new:

"We will occasionally watch a cooking show on the TV as a family, and our daughter loved seeing the judges taste the dishes and award a winner. When making a new dish that our daughter has never had before, I will often call her into the kitchen, where I have a small amount dished out, and ask her to be the judge. She will taste the dish and either provide commentary about how it needs more 'flower power' (salt), or if she likes it, she will extend her hand and give me a firm handshake and tell me 'well done.'"

Steve adds, "What matters most is that you are patient with your child. Continue to set the example for the types of foods that you wish for them to eat and encourage their curiosity. Try different techniques that works best for your family and remove stress from mealtime. This provides quality time together and encourages healthy eating habits in the future."

Well said, Steve. Well said.

The next several chapters provide recipes aimed at families of children ages twelve months and above, though younger children can enjoy many of them, too. We offer a variety of flavor profiles and textures, all of which have been kid-tested and approved. That doesn't mean that every kid who has tried these foods has liked every one, and it certainly doesn't mean your kid will either, but they all are go-tos for at least one family and were then vetted by other vegan or nonvegan kid testers, too, so we are hopeful that you will find some new favorites here.

WAKEY WAKEY

SUPERPOWER-PACKED PARFAIT

THUMBPRINT BREAKFAST COOKIES

WHITE BEAN WONDER WAFFLES

CORNMEAL AND OAT PANCAKES

CREAMY CASHEW AVOCADO TOAST

PURPLE PORRIDGE BREAKFAST POPS

PBJ SMOOTHIE BOWL

What is deemed acceptable as "breakfast food" these days is a little disturbing. Sure, bacon and eggs contain protein, along with a boatload of sodium and cholesterol. But the majority of kiddie breakfast foods are just straight up sugar: sugary cereals, pastries, donuts, sugary fruit juices from concentrate, frozen waffles with maple-flavored syrup, and really anything with white flour, which the body processes just like sugar. Throw in a glass of cow's milk or other dairy product and the host of issues they can cause (not to mention the animals who suffered before it got to your table), and we seem to be setting our kids up for problems in the future.

Whether you need something quick for the morning rush or something more relaxed and elaborate for weekends, this chapter has some ideas for breakfasts that will fuel your little one with the best of what breakfast foods have to offer: plenty of fruits, filling whole grains, and tasty proteins. This is what our breakfast chapter entails. And guess what? It's kid-approved. Go figure.

SUPERPOWER-PACKED PARFAIT

This recipe was inspired by Laura's favorite go-to, gut-healthy breakfast recipe by Robyn Youkilis, the guru of gut health. This simple and delicious breakfast is perfect for fueling your little super hero.

If you use a calcium-fortified yogurt, a serving of this parfait supplies more than 15 percent of the calcium one-to-three-year-olds need to build strong bones. That same serving also provides almost one-quarter of their daily zinc needs.

MAKES 1 LITTLE-KID SERVING

¼ cup favorite vegan yogurt

2 tablespoons rolled oats

½ teaspoon chia seeds

¼ cup blueberries or other favorite berry or fruit

¼ ripe banana, sliced (or more of another favorite fruit)

½ tablespoon nut butter (optional)

½ tablespoon Caramel Sauce (page 200), pure maple syrup, or coconut sugar (optional, if using unsweetened yogurt)

In a kids' breakfast bowl, combine the yogurt, oats, and chia seeds. Top with the berries, banana, nut butter (if using), and sweetener (if using), and serve! Alternatively, combine the ingredients and toppings in a small mason jar, seal, and refrigerate until ready to serve. It will keep for 2 to 3 days.

THUMBPRINT BREAKFAST COOKIES

What kid doesn't want a cookie at all times? These are a great make-ahead breakfast option for a busy week. One of these cookies supplies almost 30 percent of the protein recommendation for a one-to-three-year-old, along with generous amounts of iron and zinc. What a great way to start the day!

MAKES 18

2 tablespoons flax meal

1½ cups rolled oats

½ cup oat flour

½ cup almond meal (or oat flour, if making a nut-free version)

½ teaspoon baking powder

½ teaspoon baking soda

Pinch of sea salt, or to taste (see Note)

2 ripe medium bananas

½ cup natural peanut butter (substitute tahini if nut-free)

2 tablespoons coconut oil, melted, plus more for greasing, if needed

3 tablespoons pure maple syrup

1 teaspoon pure vanilla extract

About ½ cup Berry Chia Jam (page 198) or jam of choice

Preheat the oven to 350°F. Line a baking sheet with parchment paper or lightly grease with coconut oil.

In a small bowl or cup, combine the flax meal and 6 tablespoons water and refrigerate until the mixture has thickened to an "eggy" texture, about 5 minutes.

Meanwhile, in a medium bowl, whisk together the oats, oat flour, almond meal, baking powder, baking soda, and salt. Add the flax "egg" to the dry ingredients and stir until combined.

In another medium bowl, mash the bananas, then add the peanut butter, melted coconut oil, maple syrup, and vanilla and stir until well combined. Mix in the flax "egg"—flour mixture.

Drop the dough by scant ¼-cups onto the prepared baking sheet (they won't expand much). Use the back of a small spoon to gently make a "thumbprint" in the center of each cookie, then fill each thumbprint with about 1 teaspoon of the jam.

Bake until the cookies are lightly golden brown, 15 to 17 minutes. Let the cookies rest on the baking sheet for a few minutes before transferring them to a wire rack to cool completely. The cookies will last in an airtight container for 3 days at room temperature or up to 5 days in the fridge.

Note Depending on how salty your peanut butter is, you may want to use more or less salt.

WHITE BEAN WONDER WAFFLES

What do you do when your vegan toddler doesn't like beans? Put them in waffles! Marisa saw a version of these in *The Kind Mama* by Alicia Silverstone and tweaked them to be more kid-friendly. You'll need a high-powered blender to fully puree the soaked dry beans.

One quarter-waffle serving, if made with a calcium and vitamin B_{12}—fortified milk, supplies more than 15 percent of a toddler's daily calcium and one-third of the recommendation for vitamin B_{12}. The beans help the same serving provide almost 5 grams of protein, about 40 percent of the daily recommendation for toddlers.

This recipe makes a lot, so feel free to freeze what you don't eat for another day.

MAKES ABOUT 3 (ABOUT 12 SERVINGS)

½ cup dried navy beans, soaked in water overnight, drained, and rinsed thoroughly

2 cups nondairy milk

1 teaspoon pure vanilla extract

1 cup spelt flour

⅓ cup oat flour

1 tablespoon chia seeds or flax meal

Rounded ½ teaspoon ground cinnamon

1½ teaspoons baking powder

¼ teaspoon salt

Coconut oil spray or other high-heat oil spray

Optional toppings: Vegan butter, pure maple syrup, Caramel Sauce (page 200), fruit, or other toppings of your choice

Heat your waffle iron on medium-high.

In a blender, combine the beans, milk, and vanilla and blend until smooth. Add the spelt flour, oat flour, chia seeds, cinnamon, baking powder, and salt and blend again until smooth, stopping periodically to scrape down the sides and stir with a big spoon.

Spray the waffle iron plates with coconut oil. Ladle in the batter, filling the plates completely, and cook until the waffles are golden brown, about 5 minutes. Remove the waffles from the waffle iron and repeat with the remaining batter.

Top the waffles as desired. Waffles will last in an airtight container in the freezer for up to a month.

CORNMEAL AND OAT PANCAKES

Pancakes. Laura takes a lot of pride in making deliciously healthy versions of this normally nutritionally devoid breakfast item. This versatile gluten-free pancake can be made plain or with blueberries or chocolate chips, or simply topped with some vegan butter and pure maple syrup. However you like your hotcakes, this recipe will not disappoint. Just one pancake provides 10 percent of the protein, iron, magnesium, and zinc that your toddler needs.

MAKES 10 TO 12 (10 TO 12 SERVINGS)

½ cup cornmeal

1 cup oat flour

3 tablespoons flax meal

¼ teaspoon sea salt

1 cup unsweetened almond milk

½ cup unsweetened applesauce

¾ cup vegan chocolate chips
or blueberries (optional)

Coconut oil or vegan butter, for cooking

Optional toppings: Pure maple syrup, agave nectar, nut butter, vegan butter, coconut cream, Orangutan-Approved Chocolate-Hazelnut Spread (page 199), "sprinkles" (see pages 186–189), fresh fruit, nuts, hulled hemp seeds

Preheat the oven to 200°F.

In a medium bowl, whisk together the cornmeal, oat flour, flax meal, and salt. Stir in the milk and applesauce and combine. Fold in the chocolate chips (if using).

Warm a griddle or skillet over medium-low to medium heat. You want it hot but not screaming hot. Once the pan is hot, drizzle the surface with coconut oil; the oil should not smoke when added to the pan. Scoop a scant ¼ cup of the batter onto the griddle or pan for each pancake. Cook until the bottom of each pancake is golden, 3 to 4 minutes, then flip and cook for 2 to 4 minutes more. Keep the pancakes warm in the 200°F oven until ready to serve.

Top the pancakes as desired, and enjoy! These pancakes are best served fresh, but leftovers can be stored in an airtight container or bag in the fridge for up to 3 days, or in the freezer for up to a month.

CREAMY CASHEW AVOCADO TOAST

Whoever invented avocado toast deserves our undying gratitude. When Gabriel was little, he loved it paired with Dreena Burton's Cashew Chive Spread, which is a perfect way to get so much good stuff into a kiddo's body first thing in the morning. A slice of this toast delivers at least 10 percent of the iron, zinc, potassium, magnesium, vitamin C, thiamine, riboflavin, niacin, and vitamin E a one-to-eight-year-old needs daily and about a quarter of the daily recommended protein for a four-to-eight-year-old in a serving as well.

MAKES 1 SERVING

1 tablespoon Cashew Chive Spread (page 196)

1 slice whole-grain toast

2 slices ripe avocado

Cover the toast with the Cashew Chive Spread, then smoosh the avocado on top. Cut into small squares and serve.

PURPLE PORRIDGE BREAKFAST POPS

Marisa's daughter goes through phases where she only wants ice pops for breakfast. Rather than make a fuss about it, Marisa just rolled with it and made her an ice pop that included the elements of the oaty breakfast Marisa wanted her to have, proving further that sometimes kids will accept in ice pop form what they will not eat any other way. Okay then!

One ice pop made with calcium- and vitamin B_{12}—fortified nondairy milk delivers more than 30 percent of a toddler's recommended daily intake for iron, more than 20 percent of zinc, more than 15 percent of protein, more than 10 percent of calcium, and at least half the vitamin B_{12}.

MAKES 6

1 cup fresh or frozen blueberries

1 cup vanilla nondairy milk (or regular nondairy milk mixed with ⅛ teaspoon pure vanilla extract)

1 ripe banana

⅓ cup fortified baby oat cereal (or rolled oats, if you don't have cereal, but oats contain less iron)

1 tablespoon almond butter

1 teaspoon flax meal

Combine all the ingredients in a blender and blend until smooth. Pour into six ice pop molds and freeze for at least 4 hours before unmolding and serving.

PBJ SMOOTHIE BOWL

Some years ago, smoothie bowls with various colorful toppings, including fruit shapes, hit Instagram and Pinterest and almost broke the Internet. The options to decorate and personalize this delicious breakfast bowl for your unique kiddo are limitless.

This smoothie bowl's fruit supplies vitamin C—almost three-quarters of the recommended daily amount for four-to-eight-year-olds and 100 percent for one-to-three-year-olds in one serving. If you use a nondairy milk fortified with vitamin B_{12}, a serving provides at least 20 percent of a child's vitamin B_{12} needs.

MAKES 1 CUP (2 SERVINGS)

¾ cup mixed frozen berries

1 ripe banana

¼ cup fortified nondairy milk

1 tablespoon natural peanut butter

2 teaspoons Tutti-Frutti Sprinkle (page 188; optional)

In a blender, combine the berries, one-quarter of the banana, the milk, and the peanut butter and blend until smooth. Pour half the smoothie into a bowl. Top with 1 teaspoon of the Tutti-Frutti Sprinkle, if desired. Slice half of the remaining banana (see Note), arrange the slices on the smoothie, then repeat with the remaining ingredients. Serve.

Note If you have any cute small cookie cutters, slice the remaining banana lengthwise into thirds and use the cookie cutters to punch out fun shapes, then use them to garnish the smoothie bowl.

SIPS AND SLURPS

BOOSTED ALMOND MILK

NEVERLAND SMOOTHIE

PINK DRINK

CARROT-APPLE JUICE

PERFECT FIRST GREEN JUICE

SUNSET POPS

Getting our kiddos to sit down and eat plates of greens (or just food in general) can be a challenge sometimes. But these nutritious smoothies and juices cram in lots of vitamins while also being kid-approved. Secret tip: All the recipes in this chapter also freeze into delicious pops!

BOOSTED ALMOND MILK

When Marisa's son was one and self-weaned, we discovered he had a soy sensitivity. She couldn't give him soy milk, and pea milk wasn't available yet. Marisa consulted Dr. Joel Fuhrman about what to do, and he recommended making almond milk from scratch every day in the Vitamix. This recipe was inspired by his recommendation and is a great alternative to soy milk or pea milk, provided you use an almond milk that is fortified with calcium, vitamin D, and vitamin B_{12}.

Almond milk is low in some essential amino acids, so be sure that your child eats a variety of other protein sources—including legumes, whole grains, and vegetables—every day if you're using this milk as your child's primary beverage. Marisa used unsweetened almond milk and sweetened it with dates, as per Dr. Fuhrman, but you can use regular almond milk as well. You'll need to make it fresh every day because it doesn't keep overnight.

MAKES 2 CUPS (OR FOUR ½-CUP TODDLER SERVINGS)

2 tablespoons raw almonds

2 tablespoons hulled hemp seeds

2 (or more) Medjool dates, pitted

2 cups store-bought unsweetened almond milk

Combine all the ingredients in a high-powered blender and blend on high for a minute or two, until completely blended. If your child doesn't like the taste, blend in another date or two for sweetness, but you'll want the fewest number of dates that the child will accept. If you don't have a high-powered blender and there are still chunks of dates or nuts in the milk, feel free to pour the almond milk through a strainer and discard the solids.

Serve immediately, storing any extra in a jar in the fridge for use throughout the day. It will not keep overnight, so discard any you haven't used at the end of the day.

NEVERLAND SMOOTHIE

During Gabriel's Peter Pan phase, we sold this slightly tropical green smoothie pop to him as something straight out of Neverland. He bought it. Freezing it as an ice pop makes it even more fun.

A serving of this smoothie has about 100 percent of the vitamin C and one-third of the vitamin A that a one-to-five-year-old needs per day.

MAKES ABOUT 3 CUPS (4 SERVINGS)

1 cup fresh orange juice

1 cup unsweetened almond milk

1 frozen ripe banana

1 cup frozen chopped mango

1 cup lightly packed fresh spinach

Combine all the ingredients in a blender and blend until smooth. Serve immediately. Leftovers can be poured into ice pop molds and frozen for at least 4 hours before unmolding and serving.

PINK DRINK

A ½-cup serving of Pink Drink has enough vitamin C to supply the daily needs of children from one to eight years old. If you use a vitamin B_{12}—fortified coconut milk, your child will also get some vitamin B_{12}, an essential nutrient.

by Amy Bradley

MAKES 3½ CUPS (7 SERVINGS)

2 cups coconut milk (from a carton, not a can; see Notes)

2 cups frozen strawberries

½ frozen ripe banana (see Notes)

2 tablespoons Barlean's Plant Based Omega-3 Strawberry Banana Smoothie, or 1 tablespoon golden flax meal

Combine all the ingredients in a blender and blend until smooth. Serve in a clear glass to get the full pink effect! Serve immediately and feel free to freeze leftovers in popsicle molds for at least 4 hours before unmolding and serving.

Notes You can use your preferred nondairy milk here, but because coconut milk is the brightest white, it will give your Pink Drink the best color.

If you use an unfrozen banana, the drink will be less thick and more liquid.

"The Pink Drink started when Owen saw strawberry milk on the side of a soy milk carton and wanted some, but the recipe included super-sugary strawberry syrup. It needed a healthy upgrade. With a little bit of real fruit and some omega-3, we had a match to the picture on the carton!" —Amy

CARROT-APPLE JUICE

Laura discovered this magical combo while studying Nutrition for Healing at the Gerson Institute. Every day the patients and students would have a few glasses of this magical juice. It turns out that carrots are great consumed just about any way. Eaten raw, cooked, blended, or juiced: Each way makes different nutrients more available to your body. But what Laura was most excited to learn was that mixing the carrot juice with apple juice actually highlights some nutrients in the carrot that otherwise might not be absorbed by the body! And with its brilliant bright color and delicious taste, this fruit-veg combo has proven itself the perfect way to get a boatload of nutrients to your kiddos. Like all our juices and smoothies, they make great pops when you freeze them.

You can thank the carrots for the whopping dose of vitamin A that this juice supplies. A ½-cup serving has all the vitamin A that a four-to-eight-year-old needs in a day. It's a good source of potassium, too.

MAKES 2½ CUPS (5 SERVINGS)

6 carrots, unpeeled

4 small to medium apples, unpeeled, cored, and coarsely chopped

Turn on your juicer and feed in the carrots and apples, alternating between them, until everything is juiced. If you don't have a juicer, you can blend these in a high-powered blender and strain through a cheesecloth or sift through a sieve. Serve immediately. Leftover juice can be stored in a sealed mason jar in the fridge for a few hours and then shaken before being served (juice will have separated), but it can also be poured into popsicle molds for at least 4 hours before unmolding and serving.

PERFECT FIRST GREEN JUICE

Littles love to drink this green juice, but they love making it even more. Be prepared for excitement and exclamations as they help turn fruits and veggies into a nutrient-rich drink to enjoy right away. A ½-cup serving supplies all the vitamin C that your toddler or child (one to eight years old) needs in a day. Drink it with an iron-rich meal to increase iron absorption.

This recipe makes 4 cups, enough to share with exhausted parents who need an energy boost without fear of caffeine jitters.

MAKES 4 CUPS (8 SERVINGS)

2 apples, cored and coarsely chopped

4 kale leaves

6 or 7 fresh pineapple spears

½ cucumber, peeled

½ lemon, rind removed

Turn on your juicer and feed in the apples, kale, pineapple, cucumber, and lemon, alternating among them, until everything is juiced. Serve immediately and feel free to pour leftovers into popsicle molds for at least 4 hours before unmolding and serving.

SUNSET POPS

These three smoothies can be served on their own but, combined, make up the beautiful sunset colors we love on vacation in Grand Cayman. These pops taste like vacation, too. The sunset effect is made by adding and partially freezing one layer at a time, but if you're short on time, you can make a pretty, swirly pop just by adding them all together without any freezing time in between.

One Sunset Pop is an easy way to meet your toddler's daily vitamin C needs. Vitamin C supports the immune system and is an antioxidant.

MAKES 9

Teeny Colada Smoothie

1 (14-ounce) can pineapple in juice

¼ cup coconut milk

Creamysicle Smoothie

¾ cup fresh or frozen peaches

⅓ cup orange juice

¼ ripe banana

2 tablespoons coconut milk

Scant ¼ teaspoon pure vanilla extract

Strawberry Punch Smoothie

¾ cup fresh or frozen strawberries

⅓ cup fresh or frozen mango

Make the Teeny Colada Smoothie layer: Drain the pineapple, reserving the juice from the can. In a blender, combine 1 cup of the pineapple, the coconut milk, and ¼ cup of the reserved pineapple juice and blend until smooth. Fill nine ice pop molds one-third full (but don't add sticks or holders yet), then freeze for 30 minutes. (Drink any leftovers or pour into a cup and set aside to combine all leftover sunset smoothie components into one tropical smoothie.)

Make the Creamysicle Smoothie layer: Combine the peaches, orange juice, banana, coconut milk, and vanilla in a blender and blend until smooth. Remove the ice pop molds from the freezer. Pour the Creamysicle Smoothie on top of the Teeny Colada layer in one mold, filling the mold two-thirds full; if this layer breaks through the first layer (meaning it's not frozen enough), return the molds to the freezer for 10 to 15 minutes, then fill all the molds two-thirds full (don't add the sticks or holders yet). Return the molds to the freezer for 30 minutes. (Drink any leftovers or pour into a cup and set aside to combine all leftover sunset smoothie components into one tropical smoothie.)

Make the Strawberry Punch Smoothie layer: Combine the strawberries, mango, and ⅓ cup of the reserved pineapple juice in a blender and blend until smooth. Remove the ice pop molds from the freezer. Pour the Strawberry Punch Smoothie on top of the Creamysicle layer in one mold, filling it almost to the top; if this layer breaks through the second layer (meaning it's not frozen enough), return the molds to the freezer for 10 to 15 minutes, then fill all the molds almost to the top. (Drink any leftovers or pour into a cup and set aside to combine all leftover sunset smoothie components into one tropical smoothie.)

Add the sticks or holders, making sure they poke through all layers. Return to the freezer for at least 4 hours before unmolding and serving.

SNACKS!

BROCCOLI HEART AND CARROT STICKS

BAKED KALE CHIPS

CARAMEL CORN

CHOCOLATE CHIP BANANA MUFFINS

CHOCOLATE CHERRY CHIA MUFFINS

BANANA BITES

CHIA SEED PUDDING

FUDGY NUT-FREE ENERGY BITES

SNACKY SNAKES

CARAMEL APPLE "DONUT" SLICES

SIMPLE STUFFED DATE HALVES

ROASTED HERBED CHICKPEAS

One of the best perks of following a plant-based diet is that between-meal noshing is not only allowed but encouraged for growing kids. The high amount of fiber keeps the digestive system working like a well-oiled machine, so veg kids can eat more food more frequently than kids consuming the standard American diet. That fiber can also fill them up quickly at meals. Adding snacks throughout the day is an easy way to make sure they get everything they need. Obviously, it's never a great idea to give snacks too close to mealtimes if you expect them to actually eat their meals, but well-timed and well-chosen snacks are an important part of vegan kids' nutrition, especially in the toddler years, when attention spans at mealtimes are short and play sessions are frequent.

BROCCOLI HEART AND CARROT STICKS

Don't throw away those broccoli stalks! They're not only edible, but crunchy and a tad sweeter than the florets. (Marisa's children actually prefer these to florets!) This is a great way to avoid food waste, and broccoli stalks and carrots pair nicely with Cashew Chive Spread (page 196) or hummus. The broccoli adds vitamin C, and carrot sticks supply vitamin A.

Cashew Chive Spread or hummus adds protein, iron, and zinc. All in all, this is an exceptional snack.

MAKES 14 (ABOUT 3 SERVINGS)

1 broccoli stalk

1 carrot

Cashew Chive Spread (page 196) or your favorite hummus, for serving (optional)

With a vegetable peeler, remove the tough skin of the broccoli stalk. Go over the stalk several times until you get to the more tender, lighter core. Cut the stalk in half lengthwise (cut it in half crosswise first, if it's a long stalk), then cut each half into thirds for 6 sticks.

Peel the carrot, if you'd like, then cut it in half crosswise. Quarter each half lengthwise for 8 sticks.

Serve plain, with Cashew Chive Spread, or with hummus.

BAKED KALE CHIPS

A serving of these kale chips is an easy way to add B vitamins to your toddler or child's diet, thanks to the nutritional yeast. Use a brand of nutritional yeast with added vitamin B_{12} and a half-cup serving of kale chips will provide almost 30 percent of the vitamin B_{12} that a four-to-eight-year-old needs daily. This recipe is an appealing way to familiarize kids with kale, a great source of easily absorbed calcium, iron, and vitamin C.

MAKES 4½ CUPS (9 SERVINGS)

1 bunch kale, leaves stemmed and torn into large pieces (about 6 cups)

1½ tablespoons neutral-flavored oil, such as safflower, sunflower, or grapeseed oil

1 teaspoon apple cider vinegar

¼ teaspoon sea salt

1 tablespoon nutritional yeast

1 teaspoon garlic powder or onion powder

1 teaspoon smoked paprika (optional, for smokiness)

Preheat the oven to 225°F.

Pat the kale dry with a clean dish towel, then place it in a large bowl. Drizzle with the oil and vinegar and gently toss, then massage the kale with clean hands until each piece is coated. Add the salt and massage again.

Spread the kale over two baking sheets, trying to keep the pieces from touching as much as possible (you want them to have room to crisp up, not steam). Sprinkle the kale evenly with the nutritional yeast, garlic powder, and smoked paprika (if using).

Bake for 15 minutes, then stir or toss the kale a bit and return it to the oven until the kale chips are crispy, about 10 minutes more.

Remove from the oven and let cool for at least 5 minutes. Store in an airtight container at room temperature for up to 3 days.

CARAMEL CORN

Caramel Corn is a great snack for older kids (it's a potential choking hazard for toddlers). A cup of Caramel Corn provides about 20 percent of the riboflavin and more than 15 percent of the magnesium recommended for a four-to-eight-year-old. Riboflavin is a B vitamin that helps turn food into energy, while magnesium is a mineral that plays a role in muscle and nervous system function.

MAKES 8 CUPS (8 SERVINGS)

2 tablespoons coconut oil or peanut oil

⅓ cup unpopped popcorn kernels

⅛ teaspoon salt (optional)

¼ cup Caramel Sauce (page 200)

1 tablespoon Confetti Sprinkles (page 189; optional)

In a medium pot, melt the coconut oil over medium-high heat. Drop two or three popcorn kernels into the pot and cover it. When you hear the test kernels pop, remove the pot from the heat for 30 seconds. Add the rest of the kernels, shake the pot, and cover. Return the pot to the heat. Once you hear the kernels start popping, shake the pot every 30 seconds or so until the popping slows down enough that you can count to 7 or so between pops. Take the pot off the burner and wait a minute or two, until all the random pops stop. Uncover and sprinkle with the salt (if using), then stir in the Caramel Sauce. If desired, top with the Confetti Sprinkles, then serve immediately.

CHOCOLATE CHIP BANANA MUFFINS

Making a batch of muffins before entering a busy week can be a lifesaver for weekday breakfasts or quick snacks. This is your quintessential kid-friendly muffin—just sweet enough with chocolate chips that kids can't resist. Because it's allergy-friendly, this is the recipe Marisa gives teachers when they want to make muffins in class.

One of these tasty treats supplies a quarter of the vitamin E that a four-to-eight-year-old needs daily. Vitamin E is an antioxidant and immune system booster. One muffin also provides more than 10 percent of the iron, zinc, and fiber a growing child needs daily.

MAKES 12

1¾ cups spelt flour (see Notes)

2 teaspoons baking powder

½ teaspoon baking soda

¼ teaspoon salt

1½ cups mashed banana (from about 3 overripe bananas; see Notes)

⅓ cup coconut sugar

¼ cup neutral-flavored oil, such as safflower, sunflower, or grapeseed

1 teaspoon pure vanilla extract

½ cup vegan chocolate chips

Preheat the oven to 350°F. Line a 12-cup muffin tin with foil or paper liners.

In a medium bowl, whisk together the flour, baking powder, baking soda, and salt.

In a separate medium bowl, stir together the banana, sugar, oil, and vanilla to combine. Add the flour mixture to the banana mixture and stir to combine. Fold in the chocolate chips.

Spoon the batter into the prepared pan, distributing it evenly and using all the batter. Bake until a toothpick inserted into the center of a muffin comes out clean, about 20 minutes. Let the muffins cool in the pan for at least 10 minutes before serving. Store in an airtight container at room temperature or in the fridge for 3 to 5 days or in the freezer for up to a month.

Notes If spelt flour isn't available, you can use whole wheat flour.

You can substitute some unsweetened applesauce if you don't have enough ripe banana—just add enough to make 1½ cups total.

CHOCOLATE CHERRY CHIA MUFFINS

This recipe was born out of Marisa's love of alliteration and her love of the combination of cherries and chocolate. Chia makes an excellent binder in baked goods and offers an extra boost of nutrition. Cherries, chocolate, and chia provide a quarter of the iron and zinc your one-to-three-year-old needs daily—all in one muffin!

MAKES 12

2 cups fresh or frozen pitted cherries (frozen are preferred for juiciness)

1 cup almond flour

1 cup spelt flour (see Note)

¼ cup raw cacao powder or unsweetened cocoa powder

¼ cup chia seeds

¼ cup coconut sugar

2 teaspoons baking powder

½ teaspoon baking soda

¼ teaspoon salt

½ cup nondairy milk

½ cup pure maple syrup

3 tablespoons neutral-flavored oil, such as safflower, sunflower or grapeseed

1½ teaspoons pure almond extract

½ teaspoon pure vanilla extract

⅔ cup vegan chocolate chips

Preheat the oven to 350°F. Line a 12-cup muffin tin with paper liners.

In a small pot, heat the cherries over medium-low heat for about 10 minutes. They will reduce in volume quite a bit.

Meanwhile, in a medium bowl, whisk together the almond flour, spelt flour, cacao powder, chia seeds, sugar, baking powder, baking soda, and salt.

Ladle the cherries and any juice from the pot into a blender and blend until smooth, then add the cherry puree to the dry ingredients. Add the milk, maple syrup, oil, almond extract, and vanilla and mix until combined. Fold in ⅓ cup of the chocolate chips.

Spoon the batter into the prepared pan, filling each liner to the top or distributing the batter evenly. Sprinkle the remaining chocolate chips over the batter.

Bake until a toothpick inserted into the center of a muffin comes out clean, about 25 minutes. Let cool in the pan for at least 10 minutes before serving. Store in an airtight container at room temperature or in the fridge for 3 to 5 days or in the freezer for up to a month.

Note If spelt flour isn't available, you can use whole wheat flour.

BANANA BITES

Banana Bites are the perfect afternoon treat. One serving delivers more than half of the essential omega-3 fatty acid (ALA for short) that a four-to-eight-year-old needs daily. Banana Bites are high in potassium and magnesium and can help your child meet his daily fiber needs, with around 3 grams per serving (19 grams are recommended over the course of a day). Feel free to substitute raisins for the chocolate chips, for a less indulgent version.

MAKES 2 KID SERVINGS

1 tablespoon natural peanut butter or other nut butter, or an allergy-friendly substitute

1 ripe banana, sliced crossways to make rounds

2 tablespoons vegan chocolate chips

2 teaspoons hulled hemp seeds

2 tablespoons Sugar-and-Spice Sprinkle (page 188)

Spread the nut butter on half the banana slices. Press 2 or 3 chocolate chips into the nut butter.

Sprinkle each banana slice with roughly ¼ teaspoon of the hemp seeds and ¼ teaspoon of the Sugar-and-Spice Sprinkle. Cover each one with a second banana slice to make little sandwiches and serve.

CHIA SEED PUDDING

If you use a plant milk fortified with calcium and vitamin B_{12}, a ¼-cup serving of this creamy dessert can provide about 20 percent of your toddler's daily needs for calcium and 25 percent of her daily needs for vitamin B_{12}.

by Tere Fox

MAKES 1¼ CUPS (5 SERVINGS)

1 cup cashew milk or almond milk (or coconut milk, for a nut-free option)

¼ cup chia seeds

2 tablespoons agave nectar

⅛ teaspoon pure vanilla extract

Fresh fruit, for topping (optional)

In a medium bowl, combine the milk, chia seeds, agave nectar, and vanilla. Cover the bowl and place it in the fridge and allow the pudding to set for 3 hours. Stir, then portion into a bowl and top with fruit (if desired), or enjoy it on its own immediately. Freezing any uneaten portions as popsicles makes for healthy treats down the line.

"Chia seeds are a fan favorite in our home. It brings me great joy in knowing that my kids understand nutrition and have fun creating with superfoods."

—Tere

FUDGY NUT-FREE ENERGY BITES

School-safe energy bite alert! One energy bite supplies more than 10 percent of the recommendation for a one-to-three-year-old for many of the vitamins involved in energy metabolism, including thiamine, riboflavin, and vitamin B_6. Also included is a third of the daily magnesium recommendation and 10 percent of the zinc, making this a snack that you can feel good about.

MAKES 18

1 cup packed pitted Medjool dates

1⅓ cups oat flour, plus more if needed

¼ cup raw cacao powder or unsweetened cocoa powder

2 teaspoons pure vanilla extract

¼ cup pure maple syrup, plus more if needed

Pinch of sea salt (optional)

Line a baking sheet with parchment paper.

In a food processor, pulse the dates until only small bits remain or a ball forms. Scoop the dates into a bowl and set aside.

In the food processor, pulse the oat flour and cacao powder until combined. Return the dates to the processor and add the vanilla, maple syrup, and salt (if using). Process until a tacky dough forms. If it's too dry, add a little more maple syrup. If it gets too wet or sticky, add more oat flour as needed. Scoop out 1½-tablespoon portions of the dough and roll them into balls. Arrange them on the prepared baking sheet and refrigerate or freeze for at least 10 minutes to set before serving.

Serve slightly chilled or at room temperature. Store leftovers in an airtight container in the refrigerator for a week or in the freezer for up to one month.

SNACKY SNAKES

One Snacky Snake supplies more than 10 percent of a four-to-eight-year-old's daily recommended protein, along with 25 percent of his daily vitamin E, an antioxidant.

by Candice McNish

MAKES 12

½ cup almonds, cashews, pumpkin seeds, sunflower seeds, or any combo you like!

2 tablespoons quick-cooking oats

⅛ to ¼ teaspoon ground cinnamon

Pinch of salt

1 tablespoon hulled hemp seeds (or chia seeds)

2 tablespoons of your favorite nut or seed butter

10 to 12 Medjool dates, pitted

1 to 2 tablespoons pure maple syrup (optional)

2 tablespoons vegan chocolate chips (optional), or 1 tablespoon unsweetened cocoa powder (optional)

In a food processor, combine the almonds, oats, cinnamon, and salt and pulse until finely ground (the nuts usually retain some texture, but that's okay). Add the hemp seeds, nut or seed butter, and dates. Process until a dough forms. With the motor running, stream in the maple syrup (if using) until the dough comes together. If it does not, add water 1 teaspoon at a time until it does. With the motor running, add the cocoa powder if you are using that, or turn off the processor and fold in the chocolate chips if you like.

Roll the dough into 12 balls—snake lovers can roll each ball into a "snake," if desired. If the dough seems too sticky to roll, coat your hands with gluten-free oat flour (if gluten is a concern) or any flour you have on hand. Store the Snacky Snakes in an airtight container in the fridge for up to a week and in the freezer for up to a month.

"In our house, these are called 'veggie balls,' even though they contain no actual vegetables, I think because they bear a resemblance to Yves veggie balls or the Ikea ones. I will say they do contain a ton of nutrients, and I was propelled to make the recipe because Ewan is a notoriously picky eater (which may have to do with having a chef for a dad!). I wanted to ensure he was getting in some good macro- and micronutrients. The good thing about them is they are super portable and package-free, and can be made school-friendly."

—Candice

CARAMEL APPLE "DONUT" SLICES

Four slices of these caramel apple "donuts" provides your four-to-eight-year-old with one-quarter of her daily zinc need, 60 percent of magnesium, and almost 30 percent of vitamin E.

MAKES 2 SERVINGS

1 apple
8 teaspoons Caramel Sauce (page 200)
8 teaspoons Confetti Sprinkles (page 189; optional)

Using an apple corer, core the apple. Slice it crosswise into eight ¼- to ½-inch-thick slices, so the slices resemble donuts. Drizzle 1 teaspoon of the Caramel Sauce on each apple slice and top with 1 teaspoon of the Confetti Sprinkles, if you like, then serve immediately.

SIMPLE STUFFED DATE HALVES

Even a simple snack like this one can add to your child's daily nutrition. Four date halves supply about 10 percent of the protein and more than 15 percent of the potassium that a four-to-eight-year-old needs daily to thrive.

MAKES 1 SERVING

2 dates, pitted and halved lengthwise
1 teaspoon peanut butter or other nut or seed butter
¼ teaspoon hulled hemp seeds (optional)

Fill each date half with ¼ teaspoon of the peanut butter. Sprinkle the hemp seeds on top, if desired. Serve immediately, or pack in a freezer-safe container and freeze for a hot-weather treat.

ROASTED HERBED CHICKPEAS

A toddler serving (about ¼ cup) is anything but small in terms of nutritional quality. That serving provides a quarter of the protein and about 20 percent of the iron and zinc that a one-to-three-year-old needs daily.

by Annika Lundkvist

MAKES ABOUT 1½ CUPS (ABOUT 6 SERVINGS)

1 (15-ounce) can chickpeas, drained (see Note)

2 tablespoons dried parsley

1½ teaspoons ground coriander

½ teaspoon garlic powder

2 tablespoons olive oil or your preferred oil

Herb salt or sea salt (optional)

Preheat the oven to 350°F.

In a medium bowl, combine the chickpeas, parsley, coriander, garlic powder, olive oil, and salt (if using) and toss until evenly coated. Pour the chickpeas onto a baking sheet and spread them out so they are in a single layer.

Bake until golden and crispy, about 30 minutes. Serve the chickpeas whole for older toddlers, or mash them gently with a fork before serving them to a baby. Store any uneaten portions for 3 to 5 days in an airtight container in the fridge.

Note Don't discard the liquid from the can! It's known as aquafaba, and it's a surprisingly versatile ingredient that can mimic the qualities of egg whites. Pour it into a freezer-safe container and freeze it to use later in recipes like the Royal Icing on page 218.

"I craved the crispy and super-delicious falafel from one of Stockholm's best falafel joints throughout my pregnancy with my daughter. Maybe that's why she is such a big fan of chickpeas! I love to make roasted chickpeas to have as a pre-dinner nibble, and my toddler daughter took to them readily as well. Tasty and nutritious!"

—Annika

SUPER SOUPS, STUPENDOUS STEWS, AND SIDES

PEANUTTY SWEET POTATO STEW

CHICKPEAS AND STARS

CORN AND POTATO CHOWDER

SOUPER SIMPLE CAULIFLOWER SOUP

LAURA'S LOVELY LENTILS

GOLDEN SOUP

CAULIFLOWER RICE

SWEET POTATO SPELT BISCUITS

JESSIE'S ONE AND ONLY GUACAMOLE

NOOCHY CAULIFLOWER BITES

MARINATED KALE

BRILLIANT BROCCOLI

Whether served before your meal, with your meal, or even as your meal, a hearty soup or stew can go a long way. We are huge fans of making a big pot of nutrient-dense soup or stew at the beginning of the week to have on hand for easily reheated meals all week long. All the recipes in this chapter also freeze well, so if you aren't going to finish it all in a week, you can freeze the rest for an easy premade meal in a pinch.

The sides in this chapter are a great way to round out a meal with some healthy veggies.

There are more veggie recipes in the "baby" section that could easily be in this chapter, including Cashew Creamed Kale (page 79), Sweet Potato Wedges (page 94), and Green Beans and Almond Cream (page 96).

For picky toddlers and busy parents, sometimes simple works best. A "side" can be as straightforward as some cut-up cherry tomatoes, carrot sticks, raw broccoli, cucumber, bell pepper, or cubes of avocado, some quinoa drizzled with a little bit of dressing or oil, or some yogurt or cut fruit.

PEANUTTY SWEET POTATO STEW

This stew is deceivingly delicious and simple to make. A little kid portion, about ½ cup, delivers almost 20 percent of a one-to-three-year-old's recommended daily protein, vitamin A, and vitamin E.

MAKES 9 CUPS (ABOUT 18 SERVINGS)

1 tablespoon neutral-flavored oil, such as safflower, sunflower, or grapeseed

4 garlic cloves, minced

1 (1-inch) knob fresh ginger, peeled and grated

1 yellow onion, chopped

1 sweet potato, peeled and chopped into small chunks

1 (6-ounce) can tomato paste

½ cup natural no-sugar-added peanut butter

5 cups vegetable broth

2 or 3 handfuls bok choy leaves or leafy green of your choice

Fresh cilantro, for garnish (optional)

In a large pot, warm the oil over medium heat. Add the garlic and ginger and sauté until fragrant. Add the onion and cook until fragrant and starting to lightly brown. Add the sweet potato and sauté for a few minutes, being careful not to let the onions burn; add a bit more oil if the sweet potatoes or onions begin to stick to the pan. Add the tomato paste and peanut butter and stir to get everything evenly mixed as best you can. Add the broth and stir to dissolve the thick tomato-peanut paste. Bring to a boil. Add the bok choy, cover, and reduce the heat to medium low. Simmer until the sweet potatoes are very soft, about 15 minutes. Let cool slightly before serving; puree before serving for kiddos who don't like to see "stuff" in their food. Garnish with cilantro, if using. Store leftovers in an airtight container in the fridge for up to 5 days or in the freezer for up to 3 months.

CHICKPEAS AND STARS

This is our favorite replacement for a traditional chicken noodle soup, but you don't have to be sick to eat it. We'd eat this delightful soup any day. It's comforting to know that this soothing soup goes a long way toward meeting a little one's needs for protein, iron, zinc, and vitamin A. A ½-cup serving has around 30 percent of the protein and vitamin A and 15 percent of the iron and zinc a one-to-three-year-old needs daily.

MAKES 7 CUPS (14 SERVINGS)

1 tablespoon vegan butter (see Note), safflower oil, or grapeseed oil

4 or 5 celery stalks, diced

2 or 3 large carrots, diced

1 (15-ounce) can chickpeas, drained and rinsed

4 cups vegetable broth

6 ounces pasta stars (pastina) or other shape pasta of choice

Salt

Chopped fresh parsley, for garnish (optional)

In a large soup pot, heat the butter over medium heat. Add the celery and carrots and sauté until the veggies become fragrant, 3 to 5 minutes (add a dash more butter or a touch of the broth if veggies start to stick). Add the chickpeas and stir to combine with the veggies, then cook for 2 to 3 minutes. Add the broth, stir, and bring to a boil. Reduce the heat to maintain a simmer, cover, and cook for 25 minutes.

About 10 minutes before the soup is done, fill a small or medium pot about two-thirds full with water and bring to a boil. Add the pasta and cook for about 5 minutes (don't overcook the pasta, as you'll be adding it to hot soup, where it will cook further). Drain and rinse the pasta in a fine-mesh sieve and add it to the soup.

Remove the soup from the heat, stir, and season with salt. Garnish with parsley, if desired, and serve! Let leftovers cool, then store in an airtight container in the fridge for up to 5 days or in the freezer for up to 3 months.

Note We prefer the taste of vegan butter, but you can use a neutral-flavored oil.

CORN AND POTATO CHOWDER

A ½-cup serving of this hearty soup supplies about 10 percent of the daily protein and potassium a four-to-eight-year-old needs, as well as 15 percent of the vitamin A, an immune system supporter.

by Natalie Freed

MAKES 9 CUPS (18 SERVINGS)

1 tablespoon extra-virgin olive oil

1 small onion, diced

3 medium waxy potatoes, peeled and diced

2 carrots, diced

3 tablespoons vegan butter, such as Earth Balance

3 tablespoons all-purpose flour

Kernels from 3 ears fresh corn, or 3 cups frozen corn kernels (see Note)

1 cup nondairy milk

3 cups vegetable broth

½ teaspoon salt

In a large soup pot, heat the olive oil over medium-low heat. Add the onion and sauté until fragrant and starting to lightly brown, 3 to 5 minutes. Add the potatoes and carrots and cook until they just start to soften, 5 to 7 minutes.

Add the vegan butter and reduce the heat to low. Allow the butter to melt, then sprinkle the flour over all the vegetables and stir to coat. Cook to toast the flour a bit, 2 to 3 minutes. Add the corn, milk, broth, and salt. Stir and increase the heat to bring the soup to a boil. Reduce the heat to low, cover, and simmer until the vegetables are tender, about 20 minutes. Check with a fork after 10 minutes. Taste, adjust the seasoning, and serve. Store leftovers in an airtight container in the fridge for up to 5 days or in the freezer for up to 3 months.

Note I've made this with both frozen and fresh corn. Fresh is much better because you get the crunch and sweetness from the kernels, but the soup turned out fine with frozen. You just don't get that extra dimension of flavor. I would not do canned corn—it would be too mushy, especially after cooking.

Variations Here are a couple of ideas to make your soup more "grown up":

Mash some potatoes with the back of a wooden spoon before you add the corn to create a thicker, more chowderlike texture.

Add some chopped fresh parsley.

Mix in a little finely chopped canned chipotle in adobo sauce (careful, a little goes a long way!).

Sprinkle with some chopped jalapeño.

———

"When my kids were little, I always liked to be able to make one dinner that we could all eat, even if we ate it in different ways! This soup is a great example. It is perfectly wonderful as a grown-up meal with a salad and some bread, but it features chunks of cooked potato, carrot, and corn for little fingers to pick up. One and done!"

—Natalie

SOUPER SIMPLE CAULIFLOWER SOUP

With much inspiration from the home and cookbook of *The Engine 2 Diet* author Rip Esselstyn, we bring you this simple, healthy cauliflower soup. The Esselstyns told us they also add a mixed herb spice such as harissa seasoning and "a *lot* of nutritional yeast" to their cauliflower soup, which gives it more flavor depth. You can get creative in making this one your own. Sautéing onions in water or broth is an easy way to cut back on oil, but to make the recipe even simpler, you can skip sautéing the onions in broth first and just toss all the veggies in at once.

A ½-cup serving delivers 20 percent of the vitamin A that a one-to-three-year-old needs, along with more than 10 percent of the potassium recommendation and plenty of vitamin C and B vitamins.

1 large onion, chopped

½ teaspoon salt plus more for seasoning

3 cups vegetable broth, divided

1 medium potato, diced

1 medium carrot, diced

3 cups cauliflower florets (½ to 1 whole cauliflower depending on size)

2 tablespoons coconut aminos (or soy sauce or tamari)

½ cup nutritional yeast plus more for seasoning

Chopped fresh herbs for seasoning

Heat the onion, salt, and ½ cup of the broth on medium-high in a medium pot and allow to simmer until the onions get soft, about 15 to 20 minutes. Add the potato, carrot, and cauliflower as well as the rest of the broth. Bring to a boil, then turn the heat down and let it simmer for another 20 to 25 minutes, until the vegetables can be pierced easily with a fork. Add the coconut aminos and nutritional yeast and stir.

Depending on your family's taste, this soup can be served chunky, smooth, or somewhere in between. For chunky you can serve as is or just mash the veggies down a little with a potato masher. For a little less chunky, you can use an immersion blender or standard blender to blend some of the veggies. For completely smooth and creamy soup, use an immersion blender or transfer all the soup (in batches if it's hot) to a standard blender and blend until smooth. Add salt, nutritional yeast, and herbs to taste and enjoy!

LAURA'S LOVELY LENTILS

This dish is one of our favorite recipes to share with friends looking for a plant-based protein option. Laura serves these lentils at least a few times a month. This recipe makes a lot, so it's great for freezing for future meals. Laura's Lovely Lentils aren't just lovely to eat—they pack a nutritional punch. A single ½-cup serving supplies about half the protein and a third of the iron and zinc a toddler needs in a day, along with about 30 percent of the vitamin A, thanks to those carrots.

MAKES 7½ CUPS (15 SERVINGS)

1 tablespoon canola or safflower oil, plus more if needed

1 yellow onion, diced

3 celery stalks, chopped

2 carrots, or 2 handfuls of baby carrots, chopped

1 (14.5-ounce) can fire-roasted tomatoes

4 cups vegetable broth

16 ounces brown or green lentils (2 cups), rinsed

Sea salt

In a large pot, heat the canola oil over medium heat. Add the onion and sauté until fragrant and lightly caramelized, adjusting the heat and adding more oil or a splash of the broth as needed if it starts sticking to the pot. Add the celery and carrots and stir to combine. Cook for 2 to 3 minutes. Add the tomatoes and broth and stir to combine. Add the lentils and bring to a boil. Boil for a couple of minutes, then reduce the heat to maintain a simmer and cover the pot. Simmer the lentils until tender, about 45 minutes, checking them after 25 to 30 minutes. (Lentils will cook faster on certain stoves.) If there's still a lot of liquid or the lentils are not soft enough, simmer for a bit longer, then check again. Season to taste. Ladle the lentils into bowls and serve. Store leftovers for up to 5 days in the fridge and up to 3 months in the freezer.

GOLDEN SOUP

A ½-cup serving of this soup supplies all the vitamin A your one-to-three-year-old needs for an entire day.

by Shannon and Steve Kain

MAKES 5 CUPS (10 SERVINGS)

1 teaspoon olive oil, plus more for drizzling

1 onion, finely diced

Salt

2 garlic cloves, minced

1 to 2 teaspoons minced fresh ginger

½ teaspoon mild curry powder

½ teaspoon ground turmeric

4 cups chopped carrots

1½ cups vegetable broth (Better Than Bouillon mixed with water works well)

1 (13.5-ounce) can full-fat coconut milk

Black pepper

Toasted pumpkin seeds, for garnish (optional)

In a large stockpot or Dutch oven, heat the olive oil over medium-high heat. Add the onion and cook until it begins to sizzle, then add a pinch of salt and sauté until slightly translucent, 2 to 3 minutes. Add the garlic, ginger, curry powder, and turmeric and sauté for 2 minutes more, being careful not to let the garlic and ginger burn. Once the onion is lightly browned, add the carrots and broth. Reduce the heat to medium, cover, and simmer until the carrots are soft and easily pierced with a fork, 15 to 20 minutes.

Carefully transfer the soup to a blender and blend until smooth and creamy (be careful when blending hot liquids), or use an immersion stick blender to blend the soup directly in the pot. Add the coconut milk and blend, adding in water as needed to reach the desired consistency. Transfer the soup back to the pot (if necessary), season with salt and pepper, garnish with pumpkin seeds and a drizzle of olive oil if you like, and enjoy! Store in an airtight container in the fridge for 3 to 5 days or in the freezer for up to 3 months.

"Our daughter loves blended soups. We regularly serve them in our house, as it is a great way to provide a simple, tasty, and wholesome meal. Feel free to mix up the vegetables. We have done a mix of carrots, squash, and pumpkin in the past. If your child is not a fan of curry powder, omit or reduce the amount used."

—Shannon and Steve

CAULIFLOWER RICE

Seems like they're turning cauliflower into everything these days. We're fully on board because it's just so nutrient-rich and easy to disguise, and takes much less time to cook than rice. You can use either a food processor or a blender.

As the National Institutes of Health says, "Your body needs potassium for almost everything it does." A ½-cup serving of cauliflower rice contributes about 15 percent of the daily potassium that a one-to-three-year-old needs. Cauliflower rice is also an easy way to provide folate, a vitamin needed for growth and development; one serving contains 40 percent of the daily folate a one-to-three-year-old needs.

MAKES ABOUT 1½ CUPS (ABOUT 3 SERVINGS)

3 cups cauliflower florets (stems trimmed off)
2 tablespoons vegan butter or oil of your choice
Pinch of salt (optional)

If you have a food processor, pulse the florets for a few seconds until the cauliflower is broken down into pieces resembling couscous.

If you're using a blender, put the florets in the blender and add enough water to cover them, then pulse until the cauliflower is broken down into pieces resembling couscous. Drain the cauliflower rice in a sieve.

In a large saucepan, melt the butter over medium-low heat. As soon as the butter has melted, add the cauliflower pieces and cook, stirring frequently, until it reaches the desired tenderness, 5 to 8 minutes. If it doesn't seem to be getting tender enough, feel free to cook until it gets softer, adding a few tablespoons of water if needed to keep from sticking. Add salt, if using, stir, and serve! Store leftovers in an airtight container for up to 24 hours.

SWEET POTATO SPELT BISCUITS

Thanks to the sweet potatoes, just one of these biscuits supplies 30 percent of the vitamin A your one-to-three-year-old needs daily.

by Natalie Freed

MAKES 14

¼ cup coconut oil

1½ cups spelt flour

1 tablespoon baking powder

¼ teaspoon plus ⅛ teaspoon salt

1 teaspoon ground cinnamon

¼ teaspoon ground nutmeg

1 cup mashed cooked sweet potato (1 medium)

¼ cup nondairy milk

¼ cup pure maple syrup

Preheat the oven to 400°F. Line two baking sheets with parchment paper or silicone baking mats.

Put the coconut oil in the freezer while prepping the other ingredients.

Sift the flour, baking powder, salt, cinnamon, and nutmeg into a large bowl, then whisk until well blended. Cut the cold coconut oil into the dry mixture until the crumbles are the size of peas.

In a separate medium bowl, stir together the sweet potato, milk, and maple syrup with a spoon or fork until well combined. It does not need to be smooth; chunks of sweet potato are nice in the finished biscuit.

Add the wet ingredients to the dry ingredients and fold together with a spatula until there are no more dry spots, but do not overmix. The dough will be very soft and sticky. Using a 2-tablespoon scoop, place mounds of the dough on the prepared baking sheets. Bake until the bottoms of the biscuits are golden, about 20 minutes. Transfer the biscuits to a cooling rack until they are cool enough to eat. Store in an airtight container at room temperature for a day or two.

"I love these light-on-the-inside, crispy-on-the-outside drop biscuits for so many reasons! They are incredibly easy to make with only nine ingredients, and they are loved by both grown-ups and little ones! The spelt flour adds a hint of nuttiness, and the sweet potato and maple syrup make these sweeter than a normal biscuit but not as sweet as a muffin."

—Natalie

JESSIE'S ONE AND ONLY GUACAMOLE

A 2-tablespoon serving is an easy way to add antioxidants to your child's day and delivers 30 percent of the vitamin C and more than 10 percent of the vitamin E a one-to-three-year-old should have each day.

by Jessica Farnham

MAKES ABOUT 1½ CUPS (12 SERVINGS)

2 ripe large avocados

⅓ cup fresh pico de gallo (see Note)

Juice of ½ lime

¼ teaspoon salt, or to taste

Put the avocados in a bowl and smash with a fork. Add the pico de gallo, lime juice, and salt. Mix well and serve!

Note To make a quick replacement for the pico de gallo, stir together ¼ cup chopped tomato, ¼ cup chopped onion (or ½ teaspoon onion powder, for younger babies and onion-adverse kids), and ¼ cup chopped fresh cilantro (optional).

"Whenever Marisa and I meet up for a bestie vacation in Cayman, it's a given that I make my guacamole—several times a week. We put it on burritos and wraps, but the kids like it best with corn chips."

—Jessica

NOOCHY CAULIFLOWER BITES

If this recipe doesn't make your kid love cauliflower, we don't know what will. A ½-cup serving of Noochy Cauliflower Bites supplies 100 percent of the daily recommendation for thiamine, riboflavin, niacin, and vitamin B_6 for a one-to-eight-year-old. If it's made with vitamin B_{12}—fortified nutritional yeast, it will go a long way toward meeting your child's needs for that vitamin, too.

1 head cauliflower, chopped into florets

¼ cup neutral-flavored oil, such as safflower, sunflower, or grapeseed

½ cup nutritional yeast

1 teaspoon sea salt

½ teaspoon garlic powder

½ teaspoon onion powder

Preheat the oven to 425°F.

Rinse the cauliflower florets and place them in a large bowl. Add the oil and toss until the florets are coated. Add the nutritional yeast, salt, garlic powder, and onion powder and toss until fully incorporated.

Spread the cauliflower over a baking sheet and bake for 18 to 20 minutes, mixing and flipping the florets halfway through. Let cool before serving. Store in an airtight container in the fridge for up to 3 days.

MARINATED KALE

A ½-cup serving of Marinated Kale contributes about two-thirds of the vitamin C a four-to-eight-year-old needs in a day. And vitamin C helps to promote iron absorption from other foods eaten at the same meal or snack.

by Aimbriel Lasley

MAKES 7 CUPS, DEPENDING ON THE SIZE OF THE KALE BUNCH (ABOUT 14 SERVINGS)

1 bunch organic kale, leaves separated

Juice of ½ lemon

½ to 1 tablespoon nutritional yeast

1 tablespoon extra-virgin olive oil or oil of your choice (but not coconut oil)

Pink Himalayan salt or sea salt

Try to get as much moisture off the kale leaves as possible by patting them with a clean kitchen towel or paper towels or by using a salad spinner. Stem the kale leaves with a knife or by tearing the leaves from the stems with your hands; compost/discard the stems. Put the kale leaves in a bowl and add the lemon juice, ½ tablespoon nutritional yeast, and olive oil. Massage the kale with clean hands, simultaneously tearing the leaves into bite-size pieces. Keep massaging for 3 to 5 minutes. Season with salt and add more nutritional yeast as needed. Serve immediately.

Variation For more advanced palates, feel free to add nuts, seeds, dried fruit, avocado, and other veggies.

"I actually first tried marinated kale at a friend's house. From there I developed my own 'recipe' and began serving it to my family. My children absolutely LOVE marinated kale for lunch, snack, or dinner. They typically eat it plain, but sometimes I like to make it into a salad or add other things for an extra nutrient boost!"

—Aimbriel

BRILLIANT BROCCOLI

Okay, we know this title may sound presumptuous, but trust. We have turned many a picky kid into a broccoli lover asking for seconds with this recipe. We love this broccoli with pretty much everything, and often eat it covered in nutritional yeast, our Vegan Parm Sprinkle (page 186), or Peanutty Dipping Sauce (page 201). Brilliant Broccoli is a great way to add lots of vitamin C to your child's diet. A ⅓-cup serving supplies a whole day's worth of vitamin C for a one-to-three-year-old and also delivers about 20 percent of the folate that a toddler needs each day.

MAKES ABOUT 3 KID SERVINGS

1 tablespoon neutral-flavored oil, such as safflower, sunflower, or grapeseed, or 4 tablespoons vegetable broth

1 garlic clove, minced (optional)

1 (1-inch) knob fresh ginger, peeled and grated (optional)

2 cups chopped broccoli florets or baby broccoli (for best results, chop the florets lengthwise down the stem)

2 tablespoons coconut aminos, or 1 tablespoon tamari or low-sodium soy sauce plus 1 tablespoon water or vegetable broth

In a medium skillet or wok, warm the oil over medium-low heat for about 30 seconds. Add the garlic and ginger (if using) and cook until fragrant but not browning, about a minute. Add the broccoli and stir to coat with the oil. Adjust the heat and add a splash of water or broth if needed to keep the broccoli from sticking. Cook without stirring until the broccoli is starting to brown just slightly on the bottom. Give everything a good stir, add the coconut aminos, and stir again. Cook until the liquid has been absorbed and the broccoli is nicely browned, 2 to 3 minutes more. Remove from the heat, let cool for at least 2 minutes, and serve. Store any leftovers in the fridge in an airtight container for up to 3 days.

MIGHTY MAINS

SUNNYBUTTER SAMMIES

FAVORITE VEGGIE RISOTTO

MAGIC BEANS

SESAME TOFU STICKS

FAM-FAVE PIZZA

TOFU DILL BITES

SNEAKY GRILLED CHEESE

TEMPEH TACOS

KIDDIE QUESADILLAS

CLEAN-OUT-THE-FRIDGE BURGERS

BLACK BEAN–TOFU BURRITO FILLING

BAKED POTATOES, A DOZEN WAYS

These are main dishes that will likely figure prominently at dinner or at lunch, whether on the dinner table at home or packed up for school or day care.

One major perk about plant-based main dishes is that while they often feature a protein, they also might already have grains and vegetables incorporated into them. On days when you get home from work late, or you've been stuck inside with a two-year-old all afternoon and she's doing her five p.m. witching-hour meltdown thing, and you don't have the headspace to create a plethora of dishes, you can feel good that if you just manage to make the veggie burger, the pizza, or the risotto, she's still getting some veggies and whole grains. And that is a darn good feeling.

SUNNYBUTTER SAMMIES

Marisa's kids go to a nut-free school, so we're very grateful for sunflower seed butter. Sometimes we swap out the jam for banana or apple slices to change things up a bit.

A whole sandwich delivers more than half the protein a four-to-eight-year-old needs in a day, along with all the vitamin E, half the zinc, and about 30 percent of the iron.

MAKES 1 SANDWICH (1 SERVING)

2 slices of your favorite whole-grain bread, toasted, if desired

2 tablespoons sunflower seed butter or nut butter of your choice (if nuts are allowed)

1 tablespoon Berry Chia Jam (page 198)

1 teaspoon Sugar-and-Spice Sprinkle (page 188)

Spread one side of one slice of bread with the sunflower seed butter. Spread the jam on top of the sunflower seed butter, then sprinkle evenly with the Sugar-and-Spice Sprinkle. Place the second piece of bread on top and cut the sandwich into the shapes and sizes you (or your child) desire, then serve.

FAVORITE VEGGIE RISOTTO

Who says vegans can't enjoy risotto? Thanks to our all-time favorite ingredient, nutritional yeast, this recipe is just as creamy and dreamy as a risotto should be (without making us feel like we need a nap after eating it). If there's one veggie that your kiddo really loves right now (no judgment if there's only one), throw it in here and this could be a new favorite in your home. A ½-cup serving of this risotto is a delicious way to deliver 10 percent of the iron a one-to-three-year-old needs, as well as a hefty amount of B vitamins. Be sure to use a brand of nutritional yeast fortified with vitamin B_{12}.

MAKES ABOUT 2 CUPS (4 SERVINGS)

1 tablespoon neutral-flavored oil, such as safflower, sunflower, or grapeseed

2 garlic cloves

1 small or medium onion, diced

½ to 1 cup favorite veggie(s), chopped if necessary

½ cup Arborio rice

2 cups vegetable broth, plus more if needed

1 tablespoon coconut aminos or low-sodium soy sauce

1½ teaspoons white wine vinegar

½ to 1 cup nutritional yeast

¼ teaspoon salt

In a large sauté pan, heat the oil over medium-low heat. Add the garlic and onion and cook until softened. Add the veggies and cook for another minute. (Alternatively, you can add these at the end if you prefer them crunchier.) Stir in the rice and immediately pour in the broth, coconut aminos, and vinegar. Bring to a boil, then reduce the heat to maintain a simmer, cover, and cook until the rice has absorbed most of the liquid, about 30 minutes. There should be a little liquid left. If there isn't, add a splash or two of water or broth.

Stir in ½ cup of the nutritional yeast and season with salt. If the risotto seems too dry, mix in a few more tablespoons of broth until you get a creamy consistency. Add more nutritional yeast if desired. Serve and enjoy! Best if served fresh, but you can store leftovers in an airtight container in the fridge for up to 3 days or in the freezer for up to 3 months.

MAGIC BEANS

A ½-cup serving of these truly magical beans has more than half the iron one-to-three-year-olds need each day, along with more than 25 percent of their daily recommendation for iron and zinc. If the nutritional yeast you add to this recipe is fortified with vitamins B_6 and B_{12}, thiamine, riboflavin, and niacin, one serving of Magic Beans will supply most of a one-to-three-year-old's daily requirements for these vitamins.

by Sayward Rebhal

MAKES 1½ CUPS (6 SERVINGS)

1 (15-ounce) can beans, any kind, drained and rinsed

1 to 2 tablespoons olive oil, hemp oil, avocado oil, macadamia oil, or other healthy oil of your choice

1 to 3 tablespoons nutritional yeast

Tamari, Bragg Liquid Aminos, or soy sauce

Place the beans in a bowl. Drizzle with the oil. Add the nutritional yeast, then drizzle or spray with tamari to taste. Give the beans a good stir and serve! Store leftovers in an airtight container in the fridge for up to 3 days and in the freezer for up to 3 months.

"This recipe was born of pure necessity. I was in graduate school and busy busy busy, so I just needed food that was super quick and high in nutritional value, and tasted good enough to please my oh-so-picky toddler. They require no cooking, and everything comes together in under two minutes from start to serving. We got our entire preschool hooked on the stuff, and I've heard nothing but positive feedback from every parent who's ever made them. They really are magic!"

—Sayward

SESAME TOFU STICKS

We like to wow our tofu-fearing guests with these savory baked tofu sticks and perfect peanut marinade.

A kid serving of Sesame Tofu Sticks made with calcium-set tofu has about 40 percent of the calcium your little one needs daily. A serving also contains more than 30 percent of your child's daily recommended iron and zinc, so it's clear that these tofu sticks are superstars. They pair perfectly with our yummy Peanutty Dipping Sauce (page 201).

MAKES 4 OR 5 KID SERVINGS

1 teaspoon sesame oil or other high-smoke-point oil

1 (14-ounce) block extra-firm tofu, rinsed

1 tablespoon sesame oil

1½ tablespoons soy sauce, tamari, or coconut aminos

1 teaspoon rice vinegar

2 to 3 teaspoons agave nectar or sweetener of your choice

1 teaspoon ground ginger or grated fresh ginger

4 teaspoons toasted sesame seeds (optional)

Preheat the oven to 400°F. Spray or brush a baking sheet with a teaspoon of sesame oil.

Slice the block of tofu in half lengthwise to create two long, thin pieces. Wrap both pieces of the tofu in a dish towel or paper towels, set them on a plate, and set another plate on top. Place a heavy book or pot on the plate and let stand for several minutes to press out excess liquid (the longer you press the tofu, the firmer the tofu sticks will be).

Meanwhile, in a small bowl, whisk together the sesame oil, soy sauce, vinegar, agave, and ginger.

Unwrap the tofu and cut each piece into about 10 strips. Lay the tofu in a deep baking dish and pour enough of the soy sauce marinade over the tofu to cover each stick. Let the tofu marinate for about 20 minutes, turning each piece occasionally to ensure even absorption. Lay the tofu strips on the prepared baking sheet. Sprinkle with the sesame seeds, if desired. Bake for 20 minutes, then turn carefully and bake until golden and crispy, 10 to 20 minutes more.

FAM-FAVE PIZZA

We met Akua Joy when we attended the first ever Black VegFest in Brooklyn and bought some muffins from her stand. We asked about her favorite family recipes, and she told us about the pizza she makes from scratch using a sauce with tomatoes fresh off the vine and a spelt crust. Once we tested the recipes, we instantly fell in love with both the sauce (see Perfect Pizza and Pasta Sauce on page 194) and the crust. They have become our go-to crust and tomato sauce, but Marisa's son also loves this crust with Green Power Pizza Spread (page 193). You can choose your family's own adventure with your preferred sauce and toppings, too.

Thanks to our recipe tester Christa Garvey for suggesting a time-saver: doubling the recipe and, after the dough has risen, freezing half for another day. Clever! One-eighth of this crust has more than 15 percent of the daily iron a one-to-three-year-old needs. It also supplies some protein, fiber, and B vitamins. Toppings like pizza sauce, veggies, and beans will make it even more nutritious.

by Akua Joy

MAKES 1 PIZZA (8 SERVINGS)

SPELT PIZZA CRUST

3 to 4 tablespoons grapeseed oil or olive oil, plus more for greasing pan and bowl

1¾ cups organic spelt flour, plus more for dusting

½ cup organic all-purpose flour

1 (¼-ounce) packet active dry yeast (2¼ teaspoons)

2 teaspoons coconut palm sugar

1 teaspoon pink Himalayan salt or sea salt

⅔ cup very warm water

IDEAS FOR TOPPINGS

1 cup sauce of choice:
Perfect Pizza and Pasta Sauce (page 194), Green Power Pizza Spread (page 193), or Muscly Marinara (page 192)

Vegan cheese of choice:
½ to 1 cup Vegan Parm Sprinkle (page 186) or 1 to 1½ cups shredded vegan mozzarella

1 to 1½ cups of your family's favorite veggies

Preheat the oven to 450°F. Grease a pizza pan or a cookie sheet lightly with the oil (see Note).

In a large bowl, stir together the spelt flour, all-purpose flour, yeast, sugar, and salt until well blended. Add the 3 tablespoons of oil and mix well. Add the warm water and mix well.

Lightly dust the counter with flour, then turn the dough out onto the counter and knead until all the ingredients are well incorporated and it looks smooth like dough. Lightly oil a large clean bowl. Place the dough in the bowl, cover the bowl with

Continued

a dish towel, and set aside in a warm place in your kitchen to rise for at least 15 minutes (this is a good time to prepare your toppings).

Lightly dust the greased pan with flour. Turn the dough out onto the pan and dust lightly with flour as well. Use a rolling pin to evenly roll the dough out to cover the pan.

Spread your desired sauce evenly on the dough, add favorite veggies and vegan mozzarella or Vegan Parm Sprinkle (page 186), and bake until the crust is golden brown, 15 to 18 minutes. Let cool, then slice into 8 wedges and serve!

Note A cookie sheet is the kind of baking sheet without sides. If you only have a rimmed baking sheet, you can flip it over and grease the bottom instead.

"Being a very health-conscious/fit family, becoming vegan was a fairly smooth transition and inspired a lot more creativity in the kitchen. My favorite food since childhood has been pizza, so it's no wonder that was one of the first recipes I wanted to perfect. Our family's favorite toppings are sautéed portobello mushrooms, red onions, okra, and sweet peppers. Pineapple chunks are also a big hit with my family. My husband and I like to top off all those delicious toppings with a chipotle BBQ sauce. Yum!"

—Akua

TOFU DILL BITES

A quarter of this recipe supplies about half the protein and 20 percent of the iron and zinc a four-to-eight-year-old needs daily. If you use a calcium-set tofu, that same serving will contribute at least a quarter of your child's daily calcium requirement.

These tofu bites can be baked or panfried or cooked in an air fryer—we've included instructions for each cooking method.

by Jessica Schoech

MAKES 4 SERVINGS

1 (12- to 14-ounce) block extra-firm tofu, pressed (optional, but recommended) and cut into ½-inch cubes

¼ cup nutritional yeast

2 teaspoons dried dill

2 teaspoons garlic powder

¾ teaspoon salt

¼ teaspoon freshly ground black pepper

Cooking spray (optional)

Place the cubed tofu in an airtight container and sprinkle with the nutritional yeast, dill, garlic powder, salt, and pepper. Cover with the lid and shake. (Kids love this part! Alternatively, you can toss the tofu and seasonings gently in a large bowl until fully coated.)

Oven instructions: Preheat the oven to 400°F. Coat a baking sheet with cooking spray or line with parchment paper.

Place the tofu cubes on the prepared baking sheet. Bake until golden brown, about 20 minutes, flipping once after 10 minutes.

Stovetop instructions: Coat a large skillet with a light layer of cooking spray. (We prefer a cast-iron skillet, but any large skillet will do.) Heat the pan over medium-low heat. Add the tofu cubes and flip occasionally until the sides are golden brown.

Air fryer instructions: Lightly coat an air fryer basket with cooking spray. Working in batches, place the tofu cubes in the basket and air-fry on the highest setting for 8 to 10 minutes, then check to make sure the tofu is browning. Shake the basket and cook to your desired crispness, about 7 minutes more (the total cooking time will be 15 to 20 minutes).

"Our family has cooked tofu every which way you can imagine, but bite-size, poppable protein-packed bites have been the go-to snacks for my constantly on-the-go kids. (I am sure many of you can relate.) Tofu Dill Bites started simply as salt-and-pepper tofu bites, then noochy tofu bites, and the next thing you know, the boys were in the kitchen with me tossing one ingredient after the next into a bowl. And so Tofu Dill Bites were born."

—Jessica

SNEAKY GRILLED CHEESE

Kids won't even notice that this sandwich has a crunchy cruciferous veggie in it. All they'll notice is the yum! A half sandwich supplies a hefty portion of a four-to-eight-year-old's protein needs. If you use a vitamin B_{12}–rich brand of nutritional yeast, a serving has more than 100 percent of the vitamin B_{12} your child needs in a day. Serve this with Muscly Marinara (page 192) for dipping.

MAKES 4 SANDWICHES (8 SERVINGS)

½ cup grated cauliflower
½ cup shredded vegan cheddar cheese
½ cup nutritional yeast
4 tablespoons vegan butter
8 slices sourdough bread

In a medium bowl, combine the cauliflower, cheese, and nutritional yeast. Lightly butter one side of each bread slice. Spread a few heaping tablespoons of the cauliflower mixture on the unbuttered side of four slices of the bread and cover with the other slices of bread, buttered-side up.

Heat a skillet over medium heat. Place a sandwich in the pan and cook until the bread is toasted and the cheese has melted enough that the sandwich holds together, 2 to 3 minutes per side. Remove the sandwich from the pan and slice it into halves or sticks. Serve immediately. Store leftover mixture in the fridge to make fresh sandwiches for up to 3 days.

TEMPEH TACOS

One taco's worth of filling delivers around 40 percent of the daily recommended protein for a toddler and 10 percent of the iron and zinc, along with vitamin C and B vitamins. Toppings can add even more to your child's intake of important nutrients. For example, diced tomatoes add both vitamin C, which promotes iron absorption, and vitamin A. Nacho Cashew Cheese Sauce boosts vitamin B_{12} and other B vitamins, and guacamole adds vitamin E and more vitamin C.

MAKES 10

1 tablespoon neutral-flavored oil, such as safflower, sunflower, or grapeseed, plus more if needed

½ medium onion, diced

1 garlic clove, chopped

1 teaspoon ground cumin

½ teaspoon chili powder

1 teaspoon smoked paprika

½ teaspoon sea salt (optional)

1 (8-ounce) block tempeh, crumbled or diced into very small pieces

Water or vegetable broth (optional)

1 bell pepper (any color), cut into strips

2 cups chopped broccoli or baby broccoli

1 tablespoon coconut aminos, low-sodium soy sauce, or tamari

10 tortillas or taco shells

1 cup diced fresh tomatoes, for topping (optional)

1 cup shredded lettuce, for topping (optional)

Nacho Cashew Cheese Sauce (page 195), for topping (optional)

Jessie's One and Only Guacamole (page 158; optional)

In a large skillet, warm the oil over medium heat. Add the onion and garlic and cook, stirring, until tender, about 2 minutes. Add the cumin, chili powder, smoked paprika, and salt (if using) and stir. Add the tempeh to the pan and stir to combine well with the onion, garlic, and spices. Cook over medium-low until the tempeh starts to brown, about 8 minutes, adding a dash of oil or a splash of water or broth if needed to keep the tempeh from sticking to the pan. Add the bell pepper and broccoli to the pan and stir, again adding a little liquid if needed to stop things from sticking. Add the coconut aminos and give everything a good stir. Reduce the heat slightly and cook for 4 to 5 minutes more. Remove from the heat and let cool for at least 5 minutes before serving.

Fill tortillas or taco shells with the tempeh mixture and finish with tomatoes, lettuce, nacho sauce, guacamole, or any other desired toppings. Store leftover tempeh mixture in an airtight container in the fridge for up to 3 days.

KIDDIE QUESADILLAS

These quesadillas are a great way to supply protein, iron, and zinc.

MAKES 3 TO 6, DEPENDING ON TORTILLA SIZE

1 tablespoon neutral-flavored oil, such as safflower, sunflower, or grapeseed

1 medium onion, chopped

½ green (or any color) bell pepper, chopped

1 tomato, chopped

1 (15-ounce) can black beans, undrained

2 teaspoons fresh lime juice

¼ teaspoon ground cumin

½ teaspoon salt, plus more as needed

¼ teaspoon garlic powder, or 1 small garlic clove, minced

6 whole-grain tortillas or wraps

1 cup shredded vegan cheese (optional)

Olive oil spray or olive oil, for the pan

Optional toppings: Vegan sour cream, Jessie's One and Only Guacamole (see page 158), mild salsa, chopped fresh cilantro

In a large skillet, heat the oil over medium heat. Add the onion and cook until softened, 2 to 3 minutes. Add the bell pepper and tomato and cook, stirring occasionally, until they are softened a little bit, about 5 minutes. Add the black beans and the liquid from the can, the lime juice, cumin, salt, and garlic and cook, stirring occasionally, until the beans are heated through, 2 to 3 minutes. Taste and season with more salt as needed. Reduce the heat to low.

Spoon the bean mixture onto one tortilla (or blend it until smooth and then spread it over one tortilla). Sprinkle ⅓ cup of the cheese (if using) over the bean mixture, then cover it with a second tortilla. Repeat to assemble additional quesadillas.

Spray or spread a thin coating of olive oil over a medium skillet and heat over medium heat. Transfer the quesadilla to the skillet, cover, and cook until the quesadilla is heated through and the cheese has melted, usually just a couple of minutes. Flip the quesadilla with a wide spatula and cook on the second side until the tortilla is golden. Remove from the pan and let cool. Repeat to cook the remaining quesadillas.

Serve the quesadillas with the toppings of your choice. You can store leftover quesadillas in the fridge for a couple of days, but it's best to make quesadillas fresh using leftover bean mixture, which can be stored in the fridge in an airtight container for up to 3 days or in the freezer for up to 3 months.

CLEAN-OUT-THE-FRIDGE BURGERS

One of these burgers provides more than half the protein and a third of the iron, zinc, and magnesium your one-to-three-year-old needs daily.

by Sophia DeSantis

MAKES 4

¼ cup uncooked short-grain brown rice (see Notes)

½ cup dried chickpeas, soaked overnight and drained

½ cup cooked veggies (any combo; see Notes)

3 tablespoons ketchup

3 tablespoons bread crumbs (gluten-free if needed)

½ teaspoon sea salt

½ teaspoon garlic powder

⅛ to ¼ teaspoon smoked paprika

⅛ teaspoon black pepper

Toppings of your choice

Put the rice in a medium pot and fill it with water, making sure you have plenty of water so that when you add the chickpeas, it will cover them. Cover the pot with the lid ajar and bring the water to a boil, 7 to 8 minutes, depending on your stovetop. Reduce the heat to medium and cook, still partially covered, for 10 minutes more. The texture of the rice should be just beginning to get chewy—it should not be hard, but it should not be fully cooked. Add the chickpeas and cook for 8 minutes. Place the rice and chickpeas in a fine-mesh sieve and rinse with cold water. Drain well, then transfer the mixture to a food processor (make sure you've drained it well enough that there isn't any residual water in the food processor).

Add the veggies, ketchup, bread crumbs, salt, garlic powder, paprika, and pepper to the food processor and pulse until the chickpeas and veggies are broken down and well blended. You don't want it to be mush, but you want it to hold together well. Try forming a portion of the mixture into a patty—if it holds together without falling apart, it's all set. Let the mixture settle in the fridge for at least 10 minutes (overnight is even better).

Heat a griddle or skillet over medium heat. Form the chickpea-rice mixture into patties and cook on the griddle or pan until browned, 8 to 10 minutes on each side. Let cool for a bit before serving. (This will also help keep the burgers from falling apart.) Serve with all of your favorite toppings and enjoy! You can

Continued

store cooked patties in an airtight container in the fridge for 3 to 5 days, but it's best to store the patties uncooked and then cook fresh when needed. Uncooked patties can last in the freezer for up to 3 months if separated by wax paper in an airtight container. It's best to defrost them on the counter slowly. You may need to reshape a little when they defrost.

Notes Make sure you use short-grain brown rice, not long-grain. The short-grain rice gives the burgers a chewier texture and helps bind them.

You can use any veggies for these burgers—whatever you are trying to use up, leftovers from another recipe, etc. If you don't have cooked veggies, then sauté or roast some to use in this recipe.

"I created this burger based off of the meaty texture I got when I made my whole foods–based taco meat. My family loves that recipe, so I knew that I needed to create it in patty form. Making sure to balance the moisture with the dry ingredients and get a patty with that perfect texture we love took a few trials, but the end result was worth it. I love being able to use up our leftover veggies and give my family something they like to eat!"

—Sophia

BLACK BEAN–TOFU BURRITO FILLING

A ⅓-cup serving supplies more than 20 percent of the protein a toddler or young child needs daily, along with more than 10 percent of important minerals including iron, zinc, potassium, and magnesium. The tomatoes in this recipe provide vitamin C, promoting iron absorption, and this filling supplies plenty of fiber as well.

by Sharon Colombo

MAKES 6 CUPS (18 SERVINGS)

2 (15-ounce) cans black beans, drained and rinsed

1 (15-ounce) can diced tomatoes, with their juices

1 tablespoon olive oil

3 garlic cloves

1 medium onion, diced

1 bell pepper (any color), chopped

8 ounces extra-firm tofu, cut into cubes

2 teaspoons paprika

1 tablespoon ground cumin

1 teaspoon ground coriander

1 teaspoon dried oregano

¼ teaspoon cayenne pepper (optional)

1 cup cooked brown rice

¼ cup tomato paste

2 tablespoons soy sauce

1 cup fresh or frozen corn kernels

Salt and black pepper

Optional toppings: chopped green olives, salsa, and avocado

In a food processor, combine half of the black beans and all of the tomatoes with their juices and process to combine. (If you don't have a food processor, you can use a blender.)

In a large pan (we use our 5-quart sauté pan, but a large wok works, too), heat the olive oil over medium-high heat. Add the garlic and onion and cook until softened, 1 to 2 minutes. Add the bell pepper and cook until the bell pepper is tender, 5 to 7 minutes. Add the tofu, paprika, cumin, coriander, oregano, and cayenne and cook for 5 minutes more. Add the brown rice, tomato-bean mix, the remaining can of black beans, the tomato paste, soy sauce, and corn. Cook until everything is heated through and mixed completely, 5 to 10 minutes.

Season with salt and black pepper. Serve as a wrap or in a bowl garnished with olives, salsa, and avocado, if desired. Enjoy.

―――

"Many years ago, before having kids, I decided to combine a few of my favorite burrito recipes into a new favorite. Once our kids came along, it became a family favorite and was one of the first recipes we made for dinner that all four of us enjoyed. We've also made this for friends and neighbors with great success! We love to garnish it with avocado, olives, and our favorite salsa."

—Sharon

BAKED POTATOES, A DOZEN WAYS

Whenever people ask Marisa for super-easy dinner ideas, baked potatoes are always at the top of her list. Why? Because even though they can take up to an hour to bake, they are not labor-intensive, but they are filling, kid-friendly, and a great carrier for whatever you want to put on them, including leftover sauces. Here are just a few ideas:

Brilliant Broccoli (page 161) and Mac-o'-Lantern and Cheeze Sauce (page 191)

Black beans, salsa, vegan sour cream, and Jessie's One and Only Guacamole (page 158)

Diced tomatoes and Nacho Cashew Cheese Sauce (page 195)

Muscly Marinara (page 192) and Vegan Parm Sprinkle (page 186)

Canned baked beans (make sure the can is labeled "vegetarian")

Truly, the sky's the limit with how many combos you can create, although Marisa's kids like to keep theirs very simple: vegan butter and baked beans from a can. Even a meal as basic as one baked russet potato, topped with 1 teaspoon vegan butter and ⅔ cup canned vegetarian baked beans, provides more than 80 percent of the zinc and a third of the iron recommendation for a four-to-eight-year-old, along with plenty of protein. Potatoes supply vitamin C, which increases the amount of iron absorbed from a meal that features this versatile tuber.

MAKES 4

4 russet potatoes, scrubbed
Toppings of your choice

With a fork, poke a few holes in each potato. Place them directly on the rack in the oven and set the oven to 350°F (no preheating required!). Bake for 45 minutes, then poke the potatoes with a fork to see if it slides through easily. If not, bake for 10 to 15 minutes more.

Remove from the oven and allow to cool. Cut the potatoes in half, add toppings, and serve! Store any leftover potatoes undressed in foil, eco-friendly reusable wrappers, or in an airtight container in the fridge for up to 3 days.

SNEAKY SAUCES, SPREADS, AND SPRINKLES

VEGAN PARM SPRINKLE

TUTTI-FRUTTI SPRINKLE

SUGAR-AND-SPICE SPRINKLE

CONFETTI SPRINKLES

GWEEN SAUCE

MAC-O'-LANTERN AND CHEEZE SAUCE

MUSCLY MARINARA

GREEN POWER PIZZA SPREAD

PERFECT PIZZA AND PASTA SAUCE

NACHO CASHEW CHEESE SAUCE

CASHEW CHIVE SPREAD

BERRY CHIA JAM

ORANGUTAN-APPROVED CHOCOLATE-HAZELNUT SPREAD

CARAMEL SAUCE

PEANUTTY DIPPING SAUCE

Sometimes all your kid wants to eat is pasta, toast, and dessert. Trust us, we know. This doesn't make you a terrible parent, and this chapter is here to help! From yummy pasta sauces to spreads that parents and kids alike find hard to resist to easy sprinkles, these recipes actually contain nutrients!

This chapter is here to help make food more fun and delicious for kiddos, while secretly making everything healthier. (Muahahaha!)

VEGAN PARM SPRINKLE

You or your kiddos can sprinkle this yummy nooch parm over pastas, soups, salad, toast, pizza, popcorn—pretty much anything! Thanks in large part to the nutritional yeast, a 1-tablespoon serving of Vegan Parm Sprinkle supplies lots of B vitamins, including thiamine, riboflavin, niacin, and vitamin B_6. Be sure to use a vitamin B_{12}—fortified nutritional yeast and a spoonful of this sprinkle will go a long way toward meeting your child's daily needs.

MAKES 1⅔ CUPS (ABOUT 25 SERVINGS)

1 cup raw cashews

¼ cup hulled hemp seeds

1 garlic clove

½ cup nutritional yeast

1 tablespoon extra-virgin olive oil (optional)

½ to 1 teaspoon garlic powder

Sea salt (optional)

Place the cashews, hemp seeds, garlic, nutritional yeast, olive oil (if using), and garlic powder in a blender or food processor and pulse until broken down into a fine crumble (it should not be powdery or too mushy). Taste the mixture and season with salt, if desired, then pulse a few more times to incorporate. Transfer to a jar, seal, and store in the fridge for up to a month.

Confetti
Sprinkles

Confetti
Sprinkles

Confetti
Sprinkles

Vegan Parm
Sprinkle

Tutti-Frutti
Sprinkle

Confetti
Sprinkles

Sugar-and-Spice
Sprinkle

TUTTI-FRUTTI SPRINKLE

This is a fun-looking fruity sprinkle to add to smoothies, breakfast bowls, ice creams, mousses, and more! Little do the kiddos know, goji berries are a great source of antioxidants, and chia seeds are awesome for digestion.

MAKES 1 CUP (16 SERVINGS)

¾ cup unsweetened shredded coconut

2 tablespoons goji berries

2 teaspoons chia seeds

In a small bowl, stir together the coconut, goji berries, and chia seeds to combine. Transfer to a small jar, seal, and store at room temperature for up to 6 months.

SUGAR-AND-SPICE SPRINKLE

This sprinkle is great on pudding, cakes, oatmeal, and more! Laura's favorite use of this one is sprinkled on top of toast spread with vegan butter or almond butter and our Berry Chia Jam (page 198). Yum! The flaxseeds in this sweet sprinkle make it a source of ALA, an essential omega-3 fatty acid. A 1-teaspoon serving supplies about 25 percent of the ALA a one-to-three-year-old needs daily.

MAKES JUST OVER ¾ CUP (ABOUT 12 SERVINGS)

½ cup coconut sugar

¼ cup flax meal

2 teaspoons ground cinnamon

In a small bowl, stir together the sugar, flax meal, and cinnamon to combine. Transfer to a small jar, seal, and store at room temperature for up to 3 months, in the fridge for up to 6 months or in the freezer for up to a year.

CONFETTI SPRINKLES

We like to put this on Caramel Corn (page 132) or Caramel Apple "Donut" Slices (page 140), but the confetti colors can brighten up any sweet snack. It can be challenging to get enough of the essential omega-3 fatty acid ALA. The hemp seeds in these sprinkles make it easier. A 1-tablespoon serving delivers close to half of the daily ALA recommendation for four-to-eight-year-olds.

MAKES ½ CUP (8 SERVINGS)

¼ cup hulled hemp seeds

¼ cup unsweetened shredded coconut

⅛ teaspoon each of various natural food colorings (see Note)

In a small bowl, mix the hemp seeds and coconut until well combined. Decide how many colors you would like to have and divide the hemp-coconut mixture into that number of bowls. Add ⅛ teaspoon of food coloring to each bowl and mix until the color is even. For a more saturated color, add more food coloring one drop at a time, mixing thoroughly after each addition. Pour the contents of each bowl onto a baking sheet and allow to air-dry for 30 minutes. Transfer the sprinkles to a jar, seal, and store at room temperature for up to 3 months or in the fridge or freezer for up to 6 months.

Note Color Garden pastels are particularly attractive and can be found online.

GWEEN SAUCE

This pesto is, hands-down, the favorite pasta sauce of Marisa's son Gabriel. It's very versatile, so you can swap in just about any green for the cilantro or kale and just about any nut or seed for the almonds. Thanks to this recipe's nutritional yeast, a 2-tablespoon serving supplies a day's worth of many of the B vitamins—thiamine, riboflavin, niacin, vitamin B_6, and vitamin B_{12} (check the label to make sure your nutritional yeast has B_{12} since not all varieties do)—your one-to-eight-year-old needs. A serving also has more than 40 percent of the vitamin E a one-to-three-year-old needs daily. Vitamin E is an antioxidant and immune system booster.

MAKES 1 CUP (8 SERVINGS)

2 cups fresh basil leaves

1 cup fresh cilantro or kale

⅓ cup raw almonds

¼ cup olive oil

1 tablespoon fresh lemon juice

⅓ cup nutritional yeast, plus more for sprinkling

1 garlic clove, crushed and peeled

¼ teaspoon salt, or more to taste (optional; only for older kids and adults, not for babies)

In a high-powered blender or food processor, combine the basil, cilantro, almonds, olive oil, lemon juice, nutritional yeast, garlic, salt (if using), and 2 tablespoons water. Blend until the mixture is smooth and no large chunks of almonds are left.

Toss with pasta and serve, sprinkling additional nutritional yeast on top, or store in an airtight container in the fridge for up to 2 days or in the freezer for up to 3 months.

MAC-O'-LANTERN AND CHEEZE SAUCE

First came Laura's Baby Mac-o'-Lantern and Cheeze (page 82) using orzo pasta. Then, out of a need to make a cheesy sauce that can be poured over any pasta, Marisa created this one with the same main ingredients, sans pasta. This isn't only great on pasta, but also drizzled on baked potatoes with steamed broccoli or over just about any grain-and-veggie bowl. This recipe calls for pureed pumpkin, but butternut squash works, too. For a thicker sauce, be sure to use the cashews.

This sauce supplies lots of vitamin A, thanks to the pumpkin! One 3-tablespoon serving provides almost two-thirds of the vitamin A that a one-to-three-year-old needs each day. Use a nutritional yeast fortified with thiamine, riboflavin, niacin, vitamin B_6, and vitamin B_{12}, and you can meet your toddler's daily needs for all these vitamins with a single serving of sauce.

MAKES 1½ CUPS (8 SERVINGS)

⅔ cup canned or homemade pumpkin puree

¾ cup vegetable broth

¼ cup plain unsweetened soy milk or other nondairy milk (see Note)

⅔ cup nutritional yeast

2 tablespoons vegan butter, such as Earth Balance

1 tablespoon fresh lemon juice or apple cider vinegar

2 teaspoons arrowroot powder, tapioca starch, or cornstarch

½ teaspoon salt, or to taste

Heaping ¼ teaspoon yellow mustard

⅛ teaspoon ground turmeric

Handful of cashews, soaked for 2 hours if not using a high-powered blender (optional)

In a high-powered blender, combine the pumpkin, broth, soy milk, nutritional yeast, butter, lemon juice, arrowroot powder, salt, mustard, and turmeric. Blend until very smooth. For a thicker sauce, add the cashews and blend until smooth.

Transfer the sauce to a saucepan and heat over low heat, stirring frequently as it bubbles, until the sauce thickens to your desired consistency, 8 to 12 minutes. Keep in mind that it will thicken more as it cools, with the consistency of a loose pudding. Remove from the heat and let cool for a few minutes.

If you decide you want an even thicker sauce, pour it back into the blender, add more cashews, and blend again. Serve or let cool and store in an airtight container for up to 3 days in the fridge or in the freezer for up to 3 months, though it's tastiest when eaten fresh.

Note If you use a nondairy milk other than soy, the sauce won't be as thick.

MUSCLY MARINARA

Lentils are a great way to make your favorite store-bought marinara extra hearty and nutritious. A ¼-cup serving of this sauce supplies more than 10 percent of the protein an older infant or toddler needs each day. For an extra protein and iron boost, serve it over pasta made of lentils or chickpeas.

MAKES 5 CUPS (20 SERVINGS)

2 teaspoons neutral-flavored oil, such as safflower, sunflower, or grapeseed

½ white or yellow onion, diced

1 garlic clove, minced (optional)

½ cup dried red lentils (see Note), rinsed thoroughly

1½ cups vegetable broth or water

3 cups Perfect Pizza and Pasta Sauce (page 194) or 1 (24-ounce) jar of your favorite tomato sauce

In a medium saucepan, heat the oil over medium-low heat. Add the onion and garlic (if using) and stir to coat with the oil. Cook until fragrant, about 2 minutes. Add the lentils and broth and stir gently to combine.

Bring to a boil, then lower the heat to keep it to a simmer, covered, until the lentils are tender and beginning to fall apart, about 15 minutes.

Add the tomato sauce and stir to combine. Alternatively, for very little ones or kiddos who prefer sauce with no "pieces," transfer the lentils to a blender, add the tomato sauce, and blend until smooth.

Reheat gently and serve over your favorite pasta. This makes a lot—let the leftovers cool, then transfer to storage containers and freeze for up to 3 months.

Note You can use brown or green lentils instead of red, but they will need more time to soften and will not fall apart as they cook.

GREEN POWER PIZZA SPREAD

This recipe was inspired by the delicious Spinach Cashew Pizza Cheese Spread from Dreena Burton's amazing *Let Them Eat Vegan* cookbook, which is Marisa's favorite vegan family cookbook. (Her copy literally fell apart from overuse. Dreena sent a replacement copy gratis—whatta gal!) For this pizza spread, we notched up the nooch for kiddos and nixed the oregano for breastfeeding mamas, who will want to steer clear of antigalactogogue herbs, which hinder milk production. This also makes a great spread for wraps, sandwiches, and crackers.

With spinach and cashews, this pizza spread really packs a punch. A 2-tablespoon serving delivers almost half the protein a one-to-three-year-old needs daily, more than 30 percent of the zinc, and more than a quarter of the iron, along with loads of B vitamins from the nutritional yeast.

MAKES 1 CUP (8 SERVINGS)

1 cup raw cashews, soaked for 30 minutes and drained (see Note)

2 tablespoons fresh lemon juice

2 cups packed spinach leaves

1 cup nutritional yeast

1 medium garlic clove

½ teaspoon salt

2 tablespoons olive oil

⅛ teaspoon onion powder

In a blender, combine the cashews, lemon juice, spinach, nutritional yeast, garlic, salt, olive oil, and onion powder and blend until smooth, stopping occasionally to scrape down the sides. Add water 1 tablespoon at a time, if needed, to thin the mixture.

Spread on a pizza crust of your choice and top with your favorite veggies and vegan cheese. This will last in an airtight container for up to 3 days in the fridge or for up to 3 months in the freezer.

Note If you're short on time, you can skip soaking the cashews and just add ½ cup water to the blender.

PERFECT PIZZA AND PASTA SAUCE

A ¼-cup serving of this luscious sauce provides more than 10 percent of the potassium a child needs every day, thanks to all those tomatoes. This recipe also supplies B vitamins and vitamin E.

by Akua Joy

MAKES ABOUT 2⅓ CUPS (ABOUT 9 SERVINGS)

7 or 8 organic tomatoes

2 tablespoons grapeseed oil

1 medium onion, chopped

4 or 5 garlic cloves, chopped

3 to 4 tablespoons nutritional yeast

Handful of fresh basil leaves, chopped

1 teaspoon pink Himalayan salt
or sea salt

¼ teaspoon black pepper

In a food processor, pulse the tomatoes for a few seconds just to coarsely chop them—do not overprocess.

In a large saucepan, heat the grapeseed oil over medium heat. Add the onion and garlic and cook, stirring, for about 5 minutes. Add the tomatoes to the pan and cook, stirring gently, for 2 minutes. Reduce the heat to low, add the nutritional yeast, basil, salt, and pepper, and simmer until the sauce changes to an orange color, 20 to 25 minutes.

Remove from the heat, blend if you like, let cool, and serve! Store in airtight container in the fridge for 3 to 5 days or in the freezer for up to 3 months.

"I discovered my simple pasta sauce recipe when I grew tired of purchasing already-made sauces that had more than just tomatoes in them. I wanted something healthier for my family. The first or second time I attempted my sauce, I loved it, and it hasn't changed since."

—Akua

NACHO CASHEW CHEESE SAUCE

We use this yummy sauce on the Southwestern Baby Bowl (page 94); Baked Potatoes, a Dozen Ways (page 183); and Tempeh Tacos (page 176).

by Stephanie Brevik

MAKES 2 CUPS

1 cup raw cashews (see Note)

2 tablespoons fresh lemon juice

1 teaspoon paprika

1 teaspoon garlic powder

1 teaspoon onion powder

1 teaspoon salt

1 red bell pepper, chopped

¼ cup nutritional yeast

In a blender, combine the cashews, lemon juice, paprika, garlic powder, onion powder, salt, bell pepper, nutritional yeast, and ½ cup water and blend until smooth, slowly adding more water as needed or until you're happy with the consistency. Keep blending on high to warm the sauce. Store in an airtight container in the fridge for up to 5 days or freeze for up to 3 months.

Note If you have a high-powered blender like a Vitamix, just toss the cashews in as is; otherwise, soak them in warm water for at least 2 hours or preferably overnight, then drain and rinse before using.

"One of our favorite go-to meals is loaded tostadas. I appreciate that I can simply mash whichever beans I have on hand and then load them up with veggies and this equally quick nacho cheese sauce. We throw this sauce on everything. It adds an amazing amount of nutrition like healthy fats, zinc, and B_{12} to anything."

—Stephanie

CASHEW CHIVE SPREAD

Marisa fell in love with Dreena Burton's recipe and uses it on avocado toast and in Cashew Creamed Kale (page 79)—it's so delicious and versatile! A couple of tablespoons of this spread delivers more than 10 percent of the iron, 15 percent of the protein, and almost 20 percent of the zinc a growing four-to-eight-year-old needs each day. That's pretty terrific!

This spread is a raw food recipe and is similar to cream cheese in consistency. It has a delicate herb and chive flavor, though you can always add additional herbs and chives for a stronger flavor, if desired. This mixture is terrific as a spread or dip for raw veggies or breads or crackers. Also think of using it in other ways, such as for a thin base layer on a pizza crust, or to layer in lasagna noodles or pasta shells in place of cheese.

by Dreena Burton, reprinted from *Let Them Eat Vegan*

MAKES 1¾ CUPS (ABOUT 14 SERVINGS)

1¾ cup raw cashews (see Note)

3 to 3½ tablespoons freshly squeezed lemon juice

1 small to medium clove garlic

⅛ cup roughly chopped chives or green onions (green portion only)

1 tablespoon fresh dill, or ⅛ cup (packed) roughly chopped fresh basil

½ teaspoon sea salt

Freshly ground black pepper

½ cup water (plus more to thin the mixture, if needed)

2 to 3 teaspoons extra-virgin olive oil (optional)

In a food processor, combine all the ingredients (starting with 3 tablespoons of the lemon juice). Process and scrape down the bowl several times, and continue until the spread is very creamy, smooth, and thick. Taste, and if you'd like more lemony flavor, add the remaining ½ tablespoon of lemon juice. If too thick, add another few teaspoons of water, one at a time. This mixture will thicken and become denser after it has refrigerated for a day or two, so you may want to consider that when adding water to thin. Spread on bagels, toasted breads, crackers, or flatbreads, or use as a dip for veggies.

Savvy Subs and Adds: Brazil nuts are a nice substitution for some of the cashews. Try replacing ½ to ¾ cup of the raw cashews with raw Brazil nuts.

Cashew Chive
Spread

Berry Chia
Jam

Orangutan-Approved
Chocolate-Hazelnut
Spread

BERRY CHIA JAM

Store-bought jams and jellies are often packed with more sugar than fruit! So we love this homemade alternative, which can be made with any of your favorite berries. The chia seeds in this jam supply the essential omega-3 fatty acid ALA, and a 2-tablespoon serving contributes about one-quarter of the ALA a one-to-three-year-old needs daily. You ain't gonna find that in the jam you buy at the store.

MAKES 2 CUPS (16 SERVINGS)

5 cups fresh or frozen berries of your choice
½ cup pure maple syrup
4 teaspoons chia seeds

In a medium pot or saucepan, cook the berries over low-medium heat. Once the berries start to break down a little on their own, add the maple syrup and stir. Cook, stirring occasionally, until the berries break down into a thick, syrupy jam, about 30 to 45 minutes. If berries are sticking to the pot at all, reduce the heat and stir more frequently. Use a fork or spatula to mash up any chunks of berry until you reach your desired smoothness. Turn off the heat and stir in the chia seeds.

Let cool for a few minutes, then transfer the jam to a jar and let cool completely. Seal the jar and store the jam in the refrigerator for up to 2 weeks.

> Note This jam should thicken enough to be spreadable within 30 minutes to 1 hour after mixing in the chia seeds; it will thicken up more after some time in the fridge.

ORANGUTAN-APPROVED CHOCOLATE-HAZELNUT SPREAD

Most people can agree that chocolate and hazelnut make a delightful combination, but the store-bought versions of this spread contain nasty and unsustainable ingredients like palm oil (see page 7) and dairy, and they contain more sugar than hazelnuts! In our humble opinion, they don't taste nearly as good as our homemade version. Not to mention that a couple of tablespoons of this spread supply more than 60 percent of the vitamin E a four-to-eight-year-old needs daily, along with a quarter of the protein and vitamin B_6 and more than 15 percent of the recommended iron and zinc.

MAKES 1¾ CUPS (14 SERVINGS)

3 cups hazelnuts, raw or toasted

⅔ cup vegan chocolate chips

½ teaspoon sea salt

Preheat the oven to 350°F.

Pour the hazelnuts onto a large baking sheet or roasting pan. Roast raw hazelnuts for 12 to 15 minutes (be sure to check them at 10 minutes in case your oven runs hot) or toasted hazelnuts for 8 to 10 minutes. Remove from the oven and let cool for a few minutes.

In the meantime, put the chocolate in the top of a double boiler and heat gently, stirring occasionally, until melted and smooth. (Alternatively, put the chocolate in a microwave-safe bowl and microwave in 30-second increments, stirring after each, until melted and smooth.) Set aside.

Transfer the hazelnuts to a food processor or high-powered blender and pulse or blend on low, scraping down the sides as needed, until the nuts break down into a smooth, creamy paste, 2 to 10 minutes, depending on your food processor or blender (see Note).

Add the melted chocolate and salt and process until fully incorporated. Transfer to a jar, seal, and store at room temperature for up to 2 weeks or in the refrigerator for a month.

Note In most appliances, getting the hazelnuts to a creamy consistency will take the full 10 minutes. If your nuts are looking like wet sand, don't fret. We promise they will get creamy eventually.

CARAMEL SAUCE

In just a 2-tablespoon serving, this powerful sauce provides almost 75 percent of the riboflavin, more than a third of the vitamin E, and more than 15 percent of the zinc a four-to-eight-year-old needs daily.

by Rachel Filtz

MAKES ¾ CUP (6 SERVINGS)

½ cup pure maple syrup

¼ cup natural almond butter (or tahini to be nut-free)

½ teaspoon pure vanilla extract

Pinch of salt (optional)

Combine the maple syrup, almond butter, vanilla, and salt (if using) in a food processor. If you prefer a thicker sauce, refrigerate for 30 minutes or more before serving. Store in an airtight container in the fridge for up to a month.

"I love to use this simple caramel recipe with apple slices or just spread on toast—such an easy and healthy way to sweeten up a snack!"

—Rachel

PEANUTTY DIPPING SAUCE

(with nut-free option!)

We're big PB fans over here, but we're well aware that peanut allergies are very common and can be very serious. Luckily, tahini (made from ground sesame seeds) has a very similar taste in a lot of recipes. So if your kiddo or someone you're feeding has a peanut allergy, no need to skip this yummy recipe! Simply use all tahini instead of a mixture of peanut butter and tahini (so ¼ cup tahini, instead of 2 tablespoons tahini and 2 tablespoons PB).

A 2-tablespoon serving of Peanutty Dipping Sauce contributes 10 percent of the iron, more than 20 percent of the zinc, and almost a quarter of the protein a one-to-three-year-old needs in a day.

MAKES ½ CUP (4 SERVINGS)

2 tablespoons natural creamy peanut butter

2 tablespoons tahini

3 tablespoons coconut aminos, or low-sodium soy sauce or tamari

2 teaspoons rice vinegar

1 to 2 tablespoons pure maple syrup or your favorite liquid sweetener

1 teaspoon ground ginger or grated fresh ginger (optional)

Combine all the ingredients in a blender and blend until smooth. (For a thinner sauce, add a little water.)

SWEET
TREATS

BOOBIE COOKIES

MINI ALMOND BUTTER CUPS

FOUR SEASONS FRUIT CRUMBLE

CHOCOLATE CHIP "TOOHINI" COOKIES

PB CHICKPEA BLONDIES

MOMOI'S DROP COOKIES

IRON SINK COOKIES

MOO-FREE FUDGE POPS

SHAPE COOKIES FOR ANY OCCASION

ROYAL ICING

LAURA'S RUSTIC CHOCOLATE CAKE

BABY'S FIRST BIRTHDAY SMASH CAKE

MARISA'S CLASSIC NUT-FREE CUPCAKES

COCOA CREAM MOUSSE FROSTING

WHITE CHOCOLATE BUTTERCREAM FROSTING

Being a kid seems to automatically come with lots of excuses for treats. Birthday parties! Holidays! Grandma's house! Tuesdays! And so on. And while sugar does come from plants, the highly processed stuff on its own can be superfuel for illness.

This does not mean we must ban treats or that we can't enjoy baking with and for our little ones. It just means we vegucate ourselves on the best options for our families.

Enter: the Sweet Treats chapter.

Balancing sugar with fiber helps keep our kids' (and our own) blood sugar from spiking, so most of the recipes in this chapter contain fiber and/or can easily be paired with some fresh fruit for added balance (no thank you, sugar highs!). For additional balance, it is also good to serve sweet treats after a nutritious plant-based meal that's high in fiber.

For the most part, we stuck to whole plant—based ingredients in this chapter and use healthier low-glycemic sweeteners like coconut sugar, real maple syrup, and Medjool dates. That being said, we do understand that not everyone has access to all of our favorite healthier ingredients all of the time. See page 8 for a discussion of various options. We also include a few more classic vegan treats made with extremely accessible ingredients, which many folks will already have in their kitchens.

Vegan baking is near and dear to our hearts, and we wanted to make sure this chapter was accessible to all! So whether your kids are gluten-intolerant or nut-free, whether you want something extravagant or something simple, this chapter has a sweet for everyone in your family!

BOOBIE COOKIES

Even though they're meant for lactating mommies, there's no reason not to share these with the kids. One cookie supplies about 10 percent of a four-to-eight-year-old's protein and iron needs, as well as provides B vitamins like thiamine, riboflavin, and niacin.

by Jenna Matheson

MAKES 24

2 tablespoons chia seeds

2 cups organic all-purpose flour

1½ cups organic rolled oats

2 tablespoons flax meal

2 tablespoons brewer's yeast

1 cup coconut sugar

2 teaspoons baking powder

1 cup (2 sticks) vegan butter, such as Earth Balance, melted

1 teaspoon pure vanilla extract

½ cup vegan chocolate chips

OTHER FLAVOR SUGGESTIONS:

Mint essences

¼ cup dried apricots and ¼ cup macadamia nuts

¼ cup dried dates and ¼ cup pecans

¼ cup peanut butter and ¼ cup chopped peanuts

Ground cinnamon and ½ cup raisins

Preheat the oven to 350°F.

In a small bowl, stir together the chia seeds and 6 tablespoons water. Set aside until it thickens into a gel.

In a large bowl, mix together the flour, oats, flax meal, brewer's yeast, coconut sugar, and baking powder. Add the melted butter, chia seed gel, vanilla, and chocolate chips to the dry ingredients and mix well. Using a cookie scoop (1-ounce), form balls of dough and place them on a baking sheet 1 inch apart. Flatten the cookies with your palm.

Bake until the edges are lightly browned, about 15 minutes. Remove from the oven and let cool. Store in an airtight container at room temperature for up to 5 days.

"I loved gifting and eating these cookies when I had my boys. They promote lactation and are full of nutrients that a breastfeeding mother needs. They contain no processed sugar, nuts, or soy. There is a bit of flexibility with this recipe. I have included a number of different flavors, so you will never get tired of eating these cookies."

—Jenna

MINI ALMOND BUTTER CUPS
(with nut-free option)

We guarantee this one's a crowd-pleaser. Laura has been using several variations of this recipe to win over vegan skeptics for years. I mean, c'mon. Who doesn't love a nut butter cup?! One of these little guys provides about 80 percent of the magnesium and 40 percent of the riboflavin that a toddler needs per day. And without all the sugar, dairy, partially hydrogenated oils, and rain forest–destroying palm oil of the leading packaged brand! Win-win-win.

MAKES ABOUT 24 MINI OR 12 STANDARD-SIZE

6 vegan graham crackers (12 squares), ground into crumbs with a mortar and pestle or food processor

¼ cup coconut sugar

½ cup (1 stick) vegan butter, such as Earth Balance

¾ cup natural no-sugar-added almond butter or other nut butter (or tahini, for a nut-free version)

½ cup nondairy milk

1 cup vegan chocolate chips

¼ cup hulled hemp seeds or one of our sweet sprinkles (see pages 186–189), for garnish (optional)

Line a mini-muffin or standard tin with paper liners (see Note).

In a small bowl, combine the graham cracker crumbs and sugar.

In a medium pot, melt the vegan butter and almond butter together over medium-low heat, stirring to combine. Reduce the heat to low, add the crumb mixture, and stir together for a moment. Remove from the heat. Press the mixture into the prepared muffin tin, distributing it evenly among the cups.

In a small saucepan, warm the milk over medium-low heat. Add the chocolate chips and stir gently until the chocolate has melted and the mixture is smooth, reducing the heat if it begins to stick to the pan. Remove the chocolate from the heat. Cool slightly.

Gently spoon some of the chocolate over each almond butter cup and smooth the top. Garnish with hemp seeds or "sprinkles" (if using) while the chocolate is still wet. Place the muffin tin in the refrigerator for about 2 hours, or until the almond butter cups have hardened. Store in the fridge for up to 2 weeks.

Note Without liners, these treats are messy and difficult to remove from the tin.

FOUR SEASONS FRUIT CRUMBLE

Yes, we had Frankie Valli stuck in our heads the entire time we were developing this recipe. You can make this with any single fruit or fruit combination that you like! We prefer to use fruits that are in season, so we'll make this delightful dessert all year round with what's available at our local farmers' market at the time. This fruit crumble is a sweet way to add some important nutrients! One serving supplies at least 10 percent of the protein, iron, and zinc your one-to-eight-year-old needs.

Oat flour can be made at home by pulsing rolled oats in a blender for about a minute.

2½ cups chopped fresh fruit of your choice (see Note)

¼ cup oat flour (certified gluten-free, if necessary)

¼ cup coconut sugar or other granulated sugar of your choice

2 teaspoons ground cinnamon

3 tablespoons coconut oil or vegan butter (such as Earth Balance), at room temperature

1 cup rolled oats (certified gluten-free, if necessary)

Pinch of sea salt

Preheat the oven to 350°F.

Place all the ingredients in a medium bowl and mix until everything is evenly distributed. Spread the mixture into a small oven-safe skillet, cake pan, or loaf pan and bake until golden brown, about 20 minutes, stirring once about halfway through.

Serve the crisp on its own or with Cocoa Cream Mousse Frosting (page 224), vegan ice cream, or vegan yogurt. Store leftovers in an airtight container in the refrigerator for up to 3 days.

Note Mixing fresh and dried fruit together works, too.

CHOCOLATE CHIP "TOOHINI" COOKIES

When Marisa was growing up, the code word in her family for chocolate chip cookies was "CCCs." Her dad would suggest, "CCCs?" and within 30 minutes, they'd be made. This may be Laura's most tested recipe, as she felt a lot of pressure to make a CCC that was nutritious but also retained that comforting deliciousness of the classic childhood favorite. We know that putting tahini, or "toohini," as Emmie calls it, in a kiddie dessert recipe might seem unusual, but trust us, it works. Marisa's kids love their CCTCs.

One CCTC gives your one-to-five-year-old about 40 percent of the copper he needs daily. Copper helps your body use iron efficiently.

MAKES 12 TO 15

1 tablespoon flax meal

1 cup coconut sugar

½ cup tahini

4 tablespoons (½ stick) vegan butter, such as Earth Balance

1 teaspoon pure vanilla extract

1½ cups spelt flour (see Note)

½ teaspoon baking soda

½ teaspoon salt

⅓ cup vegan chocolate chips

Preheat the oven to 375°F. Line a baking sheet with parchment paper.

In a small bowl, stir together the flax meal and 3 tablespoons water to make a "flax egg." Place the bowl in the fridge to set.

In a large bowl, cream together the sugar, tahini, butter, and vanilla. Beat in the flax egg.

Sift together the flour, baking soda, and salt in a separate small bowl. Add the flour mixture to the butter mixture and beat to combine. Fold in the chocolate chips by hand.

Scoop golf ball–size portions of the dough onto the prepared baking sheet and flatten them slightly. Bake until the edges are golden, about 10 minutes. Let the cookies cool on the baking sheet for about 10 minutes, or transfer the cookies on the parchment paper to a wire rack and let cool. Store in an airtight container for up to 3 days.

Note If spelt flour isn't available, you can use all-purpose flour. You will likely need to add an extra flax egg to your batter if it seems too crumbly and dry.

PB CHICKPEA BLONDIES

Grain-free, gluten-free, and made with beans!? Yep, and it's delicious! Got B vitamins? Try one of these blondies. One square has at least 10 percent of the vitamin B_2, B_3, B_6, and folate that a toddler or child (one-to-eight-years old) needs each day.

MAKES 16

Cooking spray, coconut oil, or vegan butter, for greasing

1 (15-ounce) can chickpeas, drained and rinsed

½ cup natural peanut butter

⅓ cup pure maple syrup

2 teaspoons pure vanilla extract

½ teaspoon sea salt, plus more for sprinkling

¼ teaspoon baking powder

¼ teaspoon baking soda

⅓ cup non-dairy chocolate chips

Preheat the oven to 350°F. Lightly grease an 8-inch square baking pan with cooking spray, coconut oil, or vegan butter.

In a food processor, combine the chickpeas, peanut butter, maple syrup, vanilla, salt, baking powder, and baking soda and process until the batter is smooth. Fold in the chocolate chips by hand.

Spread the batter evenly in the prepared pan (the batter may stick to your spatula—I like to spray the spatula with cooking spray first). Bake until a toothpick inserted into the center comes out clean and the edges are a tiny bit brown, 20 to 25 minutes. The batter may look underdone, but you don't want it to dry out! Let cool in the pan on a wire rack for 20 minutes. Sprinkle with salt, then cut into 16 squares. Store in an airtight container in the fridge for up to 5 days.

Note The batter will be thick and super delicious, and since there's no raw egg to worry about, you could actually just eat it on its own!

MOMOI'S DROP COOKIES

One of Laura's first baking memories is of "helping" her grandmother Momoi (pronounced MOM-wah) paint lavender flowers on tiny delicate cookies. Momoi was an artist. Laura, then seven, wasn't quite there yet. She made a mess of a few of her grandmother's beautiful cookies. But Momoi picked Laura up, sat her on her lap, and held Laura's hands as they piped the flowers together. A true Southern lady, Momoi loved making deliciously rich foods. This recipe is a veganified version of a much less delicate but equally delicious and beloved favorite recipe of Momoi's. These cookies are impossible to mess up, so they're a great intro-to-baking activity for little ones to do with their grown-ups (with no actual baking required!).

One of these treats supplies about 10 percent of the daily protein recommendation for a one-to-three-year-old, as well as 10 percent of the zinc your child needs daily.

MAKES 24

½ cup (1 stick) vegan butter, such as Earth Balance

2 cups coconut palm sugar

¼ cup raw cacao powder

½ cup nondairy milk (preferably unsweetened)

1 teaspoon pure vanilla extract

½ cup natural no-sugar-added peanut butter

4 cups rolled oats (certified gluten-free, if necessary)

¼ cup hulled hemp seeds, for garnish (optional)

In a medium pot, melt the butter over medium heat. Stir in the sugar, cacao powder, milk, and vanilla and gently stir or whisk until combined (and your kitchen smells like heaven). Bring to a boil, then stir in the peanut butter until it is fully incorporated. Reduce the heat to low, add the oats, and stir to combine. Cook, stirring, for a few minutes to make sure the oats are fully coated. Remove the mixture from the heat.

Drop 2 heaping tablespoons of the mixture onto a baking sheet or into a muffin tin lined with liners (less messy). Sprinkle with the hemp seeds, if desired. Refrigerate the cookies for 1 to 2 hours before serving to set. The cookies will keep in a sealed container in the fridge for up to 1 week, or in the freezer for up to a month.

IRON SINK COOKIES

Many are familiar with the concept of the "kitchen sink cookie." You kinda throw anything in there: chocolate chips, raisins, toffee, potato chips—you name it! Well, we thought, what if we used that concept as an opportunity to sneak as much iron into a yummy cookie as possible?! Behold, the Iron Sink Cookies! Just one cookie has 15 percent of the iron your one-to-three-year-old needs daily. Pair it with freshly squeezed OJ or one of our vitamin C—rich smoothies to aid iron absorption.

MAKES 24

Cooking spray (optional)

1 tablespoon flax meal

1½ cups almond meal

½ cup coconut flour

½ cup rolled oats (certified gluten-free, if necessary)

Rounded ½ teaspoon sea salt

1 teaspoon baking powder

½ cup pure maple syrup

⅓ cup coconut oil, melted

2 teaspoons pure vanilla extract

¾ cup hulled raw or toasted pumpkin seeds (see Note)

½ cup no-sugar-added dried cherries or raisins

½ cup vegan dark chocolate chips

Preheat the oven to 375°F. Line a baking sheet with parchment paper or lightly grease it with cooking spray.

In a small bowl, stir together the flax meal and 3 tablespoons water to make a "flax egg." Refrigerate until the mixture gels or develops a raw-egg-like consistency, about 5 minutes.

In a medium bowl, whisk together the almond meal, coconut flour, oats, salt, and baking powder. Set aside.

In a large bowl, stir together the maple syrup, melted coconut oil, and vanilla. Remove the flax egg from the fridge and add it to the wet ingredients. Stir until fully incorporated. While stirring, begin to add the dry ingredients to the bowl with the wet ingredients, a little at a time, until completely incorporated. Fold in the pumpkin seeds, cherries, and chocolate chips (we like using a rubber spatula to do this).

Use a tablespoon to measure 2 tablespoons of the dough for each cookie onto the prepared baking sheet. These cookies won't spread much, so you can put them pretty close together. If cherries or seeds fall off, just press them back on with your hands. Bake the cookies for 10 minutes, then check on them. They should be golden brown on the edges and still feel a little bit doughy. If they're not there yet, you can bake them for a minute or two longer, but be careful not to overbake. They'll harden a bit as they cool. Store the cookies in an airtight container at room temperature for up to 5 days. Enjoy!

Note If you feel your kiddos might be weirded out by seeds in their cookies, worry not— simply grind the pumpkin seeds into a meal in a blender or food processor and add them to the flour mixture instead of folding them in with the chocolate chips and cherries.

MOO-FREE FUDGE POPS

These tasty treats aren't just empty calories. One pop provides around 10 percent of your toddler's daily recommended protein, iron, zinc, and riboflavin (vitamin B$_2$).

You'll need to chill a can of coconut milk for at least a few hours (and ideally overnight!) for this recipe, so be sure to plan ahead.

MAKES ABOUT 5

⅓ cup vegan chocolate chips

1 (13.5-ounce) can full-fat coconut milk, refrigerated overnight or for at least a few hours

3 tablespoons raw cacao powder or unsweetened cocoa powder

3 tablespoons pure maple syrup or sweetener of your choice

Put the chocolate in the top of a double boiler and heat gently, stirring occasionally, until melted and smooth. (Alternatively, put the chocolate in a microwave-safe bowl and microwave in 30-second increments, stirring after each, until melted and smooth.) Set aside.

Remove the can of coconut milk from the fridge (don't shake it!), open it, and scoop out the solid white coconut cream at the top, leaving the clear liquid behind (see Note). Place the coconut cream in a blender and add the melted chocolate, cacao powder, and maple syrup. Blend until everything is fully incorporated and smooth. Pour the mixture into ice molds and freeze for at least 6 hours before unmolding and serving.

> Note The clear liquid left over after you've scooped out the coconut cream is coconut water—store it in an airtight container in the refrigerator for up to 4 days to use in smoothies.

SHAPE COOKIES FOR ANY OCCASION

When we were kids, one of the most coveted of sweet treats was the Mrs. Fields Sugar-Butter Cookie (drool). Sort of like a shortbread cookie and a sugar cookie made a yummy baby. Here's our very own vegan sugar-butter cookie! Perfect for making holiday shape cookies or just as round cookies. These are great on their own or decorated with Royal Icing (page 218) and sprinkles (we recommend Supernatural's vegan and palm oil—free sprinkles and food coloring or our Confetti Sprinkles on page 189).

MAKES 12 TO 14

1 cup spelt flour

1 cup all-purpose flour, plus more for dusting

½ teaspoon salt

1 cup vegan butter, such as Earth Balance Buttery Sticks (see Note), at room temperature

½ cup confectioners' sugar

1 teaspoon pure vanilla extract

Preheat the oven to 325°F. Line two baking sheets with parchment paper.

In a medium bowl, whisk together the spelt flour, all-purpose flour, and salt until combined. Set aside.

In the bowl of a stand mixer fitted with the paddle attachment (or in a separate medium bowl using a fork), combine the butter and confectioners' sugar. Beat until light and fluffy, scraping down the sides as needed. Mix in the vanilla, then add the flour mixture and mix until combined. Turn the dough out onto a floured surface and form it into a ball with your hands. Place the dough between two pieces of parchment paper and roll it out to about ¼ inch thick. Place the dough in the freezer to firm, about 30 minutes.

Remove the chilled dough from the freezer. Use a cookie cutter to cut out cookies and place them on the prepared baking sheets. Return to the freezer for 20 minutes to chill.

Remove from the freezer and bake the cookies until the edges begin to turn golden brown, 15 to 20 minutes. Remove from the oven and let cool on the pans for 3 to 5 minutes before transferring to a wire rack to cool completely, if desired. Store in an airtight container at room temperature for 3 to 5 days.

Note Buttery sticks are preferable to buttery spreads when baking.

ROYAL ICING

When you have a vegan child in a classroom with a bunch of nonvegan kids, you may find yourself volunteering to bake for the class more than you normally would, just so your kid can have the same treat as everybody else. If you enter the world of holiday cookie-decorating with this recipe and any YouTube video on basic cookie decorating with royal icing, you'll be set.

This Royal Icing is intentionally a little thick for outlining the tops of the cookies first to ensure that the rest of the icing won't drip over the sides of the cookies. Also, if you are using a natural food coloring, such as Supernatural brand, which is pretty thin and watery, you'll want to start with a thicker frosting. If this frosting is too thick, or you want to thin it to "flooding consistency" for filling in the inside of the cookie outline you've already done, feel free to thin with water or nondairy milk ½ teaspoon at a time until the frosting flows more easily from the piping bag.

MAKES 1⅔ CUPS

⅓ cup aquafaba (liquid from a can of chickpeas; see Note, page 143), strained

½ teaspoon pure vanilla extract

½ teaspoon pure almond extract (or more vanilla extract, if nut-free)

4⅓ cups confectioners' sugar

Food colorings of your choice (see Note)

In the bowl of a stand mixer fitted with the whisk attachment or in a large bowl using a handheld mixer, combine the aquafaba, vanilla, and almond extract. Sift in the confectioners' sugar. Mix on low speed until the sugar is incorporated. Scrape down the sides, then mix on medium-high speed until the icing is nice and fluffy, about 3 minutes.

Divide the icing into as many bowls as you would like to have colors. Add food coloring to each bowl a tiny bit at a time until you reach your desired color saturation. Transfer to a piping bag fitted with a small round tip (use a separate bag for each color) and pipe onto cookies. Use a wider piping tip to cover larger areas and a narrower tip for details. You can also simply spread icing on the cookies with a spoon or butter knife.

Let the icing set for a couple of hours before stacking and storing the cookies.

Note We like working with natural food colorings, which contain no artificial ingredients and give nice pastel hues, but when Marisa wants a truly bright, saturated color, she uses color gels from Wilton or AmeriColor, which are vegan but do contain artificial ingredients. They have a much lower water content than natural food colorings, so they won't thin your icing. It's your call!

LAURA'S RUSTIC CHOCOLATE CAKE

If you use calcium-fortified almond milk, a cupcake (or slice of cake) will supply about 15 percent of your toddler's calcium needs. It's a respectable source of iron and zinc as well.

MAKES ONE 9-INCH ROUND CAKE, TWO 6-INCH ROUND CAKES, OR 12 CUPCAKES

1 cup unsweetened almond milk or other nondairy milk

1 teaspoon apple cider vinegar or coconut vinegar

½ teaspoon baking soda

1 tablespoon flax meal

½ cup coconut oil, at room temperature or melted

¾ cup coconut sugar

2 teaspoons pure vanilla extract

3 tablespoons pure maple syrup (optional, for added sweetness)

1 cup spelt flour

1 cup almond meal or almond flour

½ cup unsweetened cocoa powder

1 teaspoon baking powder

½ teaspoon salt

½ cup vegan chocolate chips

Preheat the oven to 350°F. Trace the bottom of your 9-inch cake pan on a piece of parchment paper with a pencil. Cut out the circle and use it to line the bottom of the pan. Grease the sides of the pan with vegan butter, oil or baking spray. (For cupcakes, line a muffin tin with paper liners.)

In a small bowl or measuring cup, combine the milk and vinegar. Add the baking soda and set aside (no need to mix yet).

In a small bowl, stir together the flax meal and 3 tablespoons water to make a "flax egg." Refrigerate until the mixture gels or develops a raw-egg-like consistency, 5 to 10 minutes.

In a large bowl using a handheld mixer or a spatula (or in the bowl of a stand mixer fitted with the paddle attachment), combine the coconut oil, sugar, vanilla, and maple syrup (if using). Mix until fully combined with no lumps.

In a medium bowl, whisk together the spelt flour, almond meal, cocoa powder, baking powder, and salt until evenly combined.

Add the flax egg to the sugar-butter mixture and stir. Add the dry ingredients to the sugar-butter mixture. Give the milk mixture a quick whisk and pour it into the bowl with the rest of the ingredients, then mix everything to combine.

Put the chocolate chips in the top of a double boiler and heat gently, stirring occasionally, until melted and smooth. (Alternatively, put the chocolate chips in a microwave-safe bowl and microwave in 30-second increments, stirring after each, until melted and smooth.) Pour the melted chocolate into the batter and mix until fully incorporated.

Pour the batter into the prepared pan(s). For a 9-inch cake, bake for 20 to 25 minutes, until a toothpick inserted in the center comes out clean. For two 6-inch cakes, bake for 30 to 35 minutes. For cupcakes, bake for 18 to 25 minutes. Let cool completely in the pan or muffin tin. To remove the cake from the pan, put a plate or cake board on top of the cake, then flip it over. If it's not coming out of the pan, flip it back up and take a knife and cut all the way around in the space between the cake and the pan, then try again. Once removed from the pan, frost as desired. If crumbly, chill before frosting.

BABY'S FIRST BIRTHDAY SMASH CAKE

You can use this cake for any occasion, but we know that many parents like to do a "smash cake" for their little's first birthday, so we wanted a delicious, naturally sweetened, baby-safe cake that we'd feel comfortable telling you to go ahead and let your baby smash and devour. Dates are a wonderful way to sweeten a cake without overwhelming your baby's system, which may be new to sugar. One cupcake or slice of cake supplies about one-quarter of your one-year-old's daily protein needs. And that's not all! That same cupcake or slice of cake has at least 10 percent of your toddler's daily recommended calcium, iron, zinc, thiamine, riboflavin, niacin, vitamin B_6, and vitamin E.

MAKES ONE 9-INCH ROUND CAKE, TWO 6-INCH CAKE ROUNDS, OR 12 CUPCAKES

1⅓ cup chopped pitted Medjool dates (about 12 large)

½ teaspoon baking soda

½ cup hot water

2 tablespoons flax meal

1 cup almond flour

½ cup coconut flour

½ cup oat flour

3 tablespoons coconut sugar

1 teaspoon baking powder

½ teaspoon salt

2 teaspoons pure vanilla extract

⅓ cup coconut oil, melted

Preheat the oven to 350°F. Trace the bottom of a 9-inch cake pan on a piece of parchment paper. Cut out the circle and use it to line the bottom of the pan. Grease the sides of the pan with vegan butter, oil, or baking spray. (For cupcakes, line a muffin tin with paper liners.)

Place the dates and baking soda in a small bowl. Add the hot water and stir to dissolve the baking soda. Let sit for 15 minutes.

In a separate small bowl, whisk together the flax meal and 6 tablespoons water to make a "flax egg." Refrigerate until the mixture gels or develops a raw-egg-like consistency, at least 5 minutes. Transfer the dates and their soaking liquid to a food processor or blender and puree until broken down into a paste. Set aside.

In a medium bowl, whisk together the almond flour, coconut flour, oat flour, sugar, baking powder, and salt until combined.

In a large bowl, stir together the date paste, flax egg, vanilla, and melted coconut oil until combined. Add the dry mixture to the wet mixture and stir until combined. It will look more like cookie dough than cake batter—do not freak out. It's supposed to look like that. Pour the batter into the prepared pan(s). Spread it out to fill the pan(s) and smooth the surface. Bake until a toothpick inserted into the center of the cake comes out clean, 20 to 25 minutes for 9-inch rounds, 30 minutes for 6-inch rounds, or 18 to 20 minutes for cupcakes.

Remove from the oven and let cool in the pan or muffin tin. To remove the cake from the pan, put a plate or cake board on top of the cake, then flip it over. If it doesn't come out of the pan, flip it back and cut all the way around the cake, then try again. Remove the pan and the parchment paper. Frost as desired. Store covered in the fridge for up to 3 days.

MARISA'S CLASSIC NUT-FREE CUPCAKES

This is no health food; this is Marisa's go-to whenever she wants a vegan version of a classic birthday cake—for school, kids parties, etc. This recipe calls for coconut vinegar, which has a wonderful malty, buttery flavor, but you can use distilled white or apple cider vinegar instead. Double the recipe for a proper double-layer 9-inch cake with a layer of frosting in the middle or for a triple-layer 6-inch cake with frosting between the layers.

MAKES 12 CUPCAKES OR ONE 9-INCH ROUND CAKE

½ cup nondairy milk

½ cup full-fat canned coconut milk

2 teaspoons coconut vinegar, distilled white vinegar, or apple cider vinegar

1¾ cups all-purpose flour

1 cup sugar

2 teaspoons baking powder

¼ teaspoon baking soda

Heaping ¼ teaspoon salt

⅓ cup neutral-flavored oil, such as safflower, sunflower, or grapeseed

1 tablespoon pure vanilla extract

Preheat the oven to 350°F. Trace the bottom of your 9-inch cake pan on a piece of parchment paper. Cut out the circle and use it to line the bottom of the pan. Grease the sides of the pan with vegan butter, oil, or baking spray. (For cupcakes, line a muffin tin with paper liner.)

In a small bowl, stir together the nondairy milk and the coconut milk, then add the vinegar and stir to combine. Set aside.

In a large bowl, sift together the flour, sugar, baking powder, baking soda, and salt.

In a separate medium bowl, stir together the milk mixture, oil, and vanilla until well combined. Add the wet ingredients to the dry ingredients and mix with a hand mixer until just combined. Do not overmix.

Pour the batter into the prepared pan or fill the liners three-quarters full. Bake until a toothpick inserted into the center of the cake or cupcakes comes out clean, and the edges are golden, 25 minutes for a round cake or 22 minutes for cupcakes.

Let cool completely in the pan or muffin tin. To remove the cake from the pan, put a plate or cake board on top of the cake, then flip it over. If it doesn't come out of the pan, flip it back and cut all the way around the cake, then flip again. Remove the pan and the parchment paper. Using a long, serrated knife, cut off the domed top (no need to do this if you're making cupcakes), then frost the cake or cupcakes as desired.

Note You can mix the cut-off domed top with any leftover frosting, then roll it into cake balls, which freeze well as a sweet treat. Yum!

COCOA CREAM MOUSSE FROSTING

For a traditional coconut whipped cream, you can make this recipe minus the cocoa powder. The chocolate adds a wonderful thickness to the cream that makes it excellent to use as cake frosting! But it also works wonderfully on its own, with fresh berries or dusted with our Sugar-and-Spice Sprinkle (page 188). Deeevine!

You'll need to chill a can of coconut milk overnight for this recipe, so be sure to plan ahead.

MAKES 1½ CUPS, ENOUGH FOR
1 (9-INCH) CAKE LAYER

1 (13.5-ounce) can full-fat coconut milk, refrigerated overnight or for at least a few hours

2 to 3 tablespoons pure maple syrup or confectioner's sugar

1 teaspoon pure vanilla extract

½ cup unsweetened cocoa powder

Remove the can of coconut milk from the fridge (try not to shake it around too much). Open the can and scoop out the solid white coconut cream at the top, leaving the clear liquid behind (see Note, page 215). Place the coconut cream in the bowl of a stand mixer, fitted with the whisk attachment. Add the maple syrup, vanilla, and cocoa powder and blend until smooth, stopping occasionally to scrape down the sides as needed. Transfer to a jar or another airtight container and refrigerate to firm up. For easier piping, refrigerate for 30 minutes to an hour and then work quickly so the heat from your hand doesn't melt the frosting in the piping bag too much. This will keep in the fridge up to a week.

WHITE CHOCOLATE BUTTERCREAM FROSTING

Really tasty vegan frosting recipes abound in cookbooks and on the interwebs, but it's rare to find any that aren't chock-full of palm oil shortening and still pipe easily onto a cake or cupcake. This one is very sweet, but empirical evidence tells us that children like very sweet. Once your children taste it, you will likely deal with pleas to lick any beaters or bowls involved in the making of this recipe. This is enough frosting to frost one 9-inch cake layer or 12 cupcakes. For a double 9-inch layer cake, double the recipe.

You'll need to chill a can of coconut milk overnight for this recipe, so be sure to plan ahead.

MAKES 2½ CUPS

¼ cup chopped edible nondeodorized cocoa (or cacao) butter

½ cup (1 stick) Earth Balance Vegan Buttery Sticks, cut into pieces, room temperature

1 (13.5-ounce) can full-fat coconut milk, refrigerated overnight or for at least a few hours

2 teaspoons pure vanilla extract

3 cups confectioners' sugar, sifted

In a small saucepan, slowly melt the cocoa butter over low heat, stirring continuously, until it has melted, 4 to 5 minutes. Remove from the heat and let cool to room temperature. (You must fully cool the cocoa butter, or the frosting will be a runny mess.)

Put the vegan butter in a large bowl. Remove the can of coconut milk from the fridge (don't shake it!), open it, and scoop out ¼ cup of the solid white coconut cream at the top, leaving the clear liquid behind (see Note, page 215). Add the coconut cream to the bowl with the butter. Whisk to combine. Add the vanilla and the confectioners' sugar, 1 cup at a time, and mix until it's fluffed up, 1 to 2 minutes. With the mixer running, slowly pour the melted cocoa butter down the side of the bowl and mix until combined, stopping to scrape down the bowl as needed. Do not overmix or it will get stiff.

Use immediately.

GUEST CHEFS

Amy and Owen Bradley live with their vegan family in Columbus, Ohio, where they bake (very) often, advocate for animals, and enjoy (too many) chocolates. Amy created the *Vegan Fam in Cow Town* podcast, which frequently features Owen and the other family members, even the doggies!

Insta: @fam_vegan
facebook.com/
cowtownveganfam

Stephanie Brevik lives in Phoenix and has been vegan for five years. She loves cooking and creating vegan dishes with her sous chef/son, Dylan. They have so much fun veganizing comfort food classics, and even more fun eating them!

Insta: @comfortfoodvegan

Dreena Burton is a pioneering vegan cookbook author and mother to three "weegans." Dreena is reputed for having reliable, delicious, wholesome recipes. Dreena has five solo cookbooks, including the popular *Plant-Powered Families*, and two titles coauthored with Dr. Neal Barnard.

Insta: @dreenaburton
dreenaburton.com

Sharon Colombo and her husband, Pete, have been vegan for nine years. They are proud to be raising their six-year-old identical twin daughters, Greta and Ursula, with a plant-powered vegan diet. Sharon runs her own web design and development business and especially enjoys supporting vegan businesses and nonprofits. They live in Portland, Oregon.

vocalvegan.com

Sophia DeSantis is the author of *Veggies Don't Bite*. She uses whole food ingredients to create plant-based recipes that will change the way your entire family views healthy food. When she's not creating magic in her kitchen, she helps real-life busy people organize their meals without tearing their hair out.

Insta: @veggiesdontbite
veggiesdontbite.com

Jessica Farnham is Marisa's best friend and lives in Novato, California. When she isn't making killer guacamole (see page 158), she does triathlons and takes care of her veg animal-lover son, Brayden, three stepchildren, and two dogs with her wife, Leigh.

Rachel Filtz is an M.Ed. graduate of the Institute for Humane Education, where she studied empathy development in children. When she's not teaching in schools or working as a pet therapy coordinator, she teaches the Kind Cooking with Kids program, which she developed. She lives with her son, Jacob, in San Diego, California.

Insta: @kindcookingwithkids

Kendra Fitzgerald is Marisa's personal trainer and friend who is the cofounder of *Devoted Mamas*, teaching prenatal and postpartum moms in New Jersey and online. She's also the founder of Barefoot Tiger, a NYC-based in-home fitness concierge company. Her most important job, though, is being mom to her sons, Liam and Aidan.

Insta: @devotedmamas
@barefoottiger
DevotedMamas.com
BarefootTiger.com

Tere Fox is the co-creator/owner and executive chef of the famed Rockin' Raw, masters of raw food on the East Coast. Her catering company, Jam, offers raw and cooked foods, focusing on gluten-free cakes and pastries for all occasions. She is also a proud mama of two vegan children, ages five and seven.

Insta: @rockinraw
@jamcakeryNYC
rockinraw.com

Natalie Freed worked as a writer/director at *Entertainment Tonight* and the *Rachael Ray Show* before becoming an at-home mom. She left television and studied health-supportive cooking at the Natural Gourmet Institute and currently lives in Los Angeles with her husband and two children, and writes a blog.

Insta: @mysourcelife
MySourceLife.com

Akua Joy is a full-time home-schooling mother of two beautiful girls (and counting) and wife to her magnificent fitness coach/massage therapist husband, Guru. Together, they run an online fitness business, Morphit 4 Life, and live in New York City.

Insta: @morphitmamas
@morphitakua
morphit4life.com

Shannon and Steve Kain live in Maryland with their sweet five-year-old daughter and a cuddly dog. They have enjoyed trying a plethora of vegan recipes, planning their vegan wedding, and welcoming a child into their plant-based family.

Aimbriel Lasley, an Indianapolis native, is committed to the health and wellness of her family. She enjoys trying new recipes, restaurants, and products (all vegan and cruelty-free) to show other families that this lifestyle change does not have to be difficult.

Insta: @black_mamavegan
blackmamavegan.com

Annika Lundkvist is a photographer and writer who specializes in a plant-based food focus and the vegan paradigm shift. She founded the digital platform *Pacific Roots Magazine*. Originally from the US, she now lives in Scandinavia with her husband and their two children.

Insta: @pacificrootsmagazine
pacificrootsmagazine.com

Jenna Matheson is an Australian mother of two energetic boys currently residing in New York. She enjoys creating plant-based foods and shares her cooking experience and creations through her blog.

Insta: @planttucker
planttucker.com

Candice McNish is a passionate molecular geneticist dedicated to a vegan lifestyle and eco-conscious living. She lives in Toronto with her husband, world-renowned vegan chef Doug McNish, and four-year-old son, Ewan.

Christina and Pulin Modi and their son, Satya, live in the Washington, DC, area, where they enjoy hanging out with their cats, fighting for social justice issues, and all things Dora and Daniel Tiger.

Lisa Pitman is a long-time vegan and author of *The DIY Vegan Cookbook*. Daily, her kitchen creativity is put to the test nourishing her two busy vegan toddlers.

Sayward Rebhal is a mother, science educator, activist, and avid urban farmer. She has been vegan for more than ten years and is the author of *Vegan Pregnancy Survival Guide*, as well as the green lifestyle blog *Bonzai Aphrodite*. She lives in Santa Barbara, California, with her son, Waits; a sweet and stubborn pit bull; two very eccentric half-hairless cats; and a cuddly snake named Percy.

Insta: @sayward
bonzaiaphrodite.com

Jessica Schoech founded Vegan Street Fair, the largest vegan event in the world, and has since created spin-off events to spread veganism in as many ways as she possibly can. She, her vegan husband, and two vegan-since-birth boys are all involved in Vegan Street Fair in one way or another, and it brings her the most joy to share this with the people she loves the most.

Insta: @veganstreetfair
veganstreetfair.com

Leinana Two Moons is the author of the cookbook, *Baconish*, which is all about vegan bacon. Her writing and photography have appeared in *LAIKA* and *VegNews* magazines. She lives in Long Island City, New York, with her husband and two children, who are all vegan.

Insta: @vegangoodthings

Many thanks to our *Vegucated Family Table* models: London Frede, Zora Frede, Cora Kolesky, Giana Matkovich, Elyse Squires, Owen Squires, Baird Todd, and Estelle Woodbury.

INDEX

Library of Congress Cataloging-in-Publication Data
    Names: Wolfson, Marisa Miller, author. | Delhauer, Laura, author. |
        Kunkel, Erin, photographer.
    Title: The Vegucated family table : irresistible vegan recipes and
        proven tips for feeding plant-powered babies, toddlers,
        and kids /Marisa Miller Wolfson and Laura Delhauer ;
        photographs by Erin Kunkel.
    Description: First edition. | California : Ten Speed Press, [2020] |
        Includes bibliographical references and index.
    Identifiers: LCCN 2019057722 | ISBN 9781984857170 (trade paperback) |
        ISBN 9781984857187 (epub)
    Subjects: LCSH: Vegan cooking. | Cooking for children. | Baby foods. |
        LCGFT: Cookbooks.
    Classification: LCC TX837 .W835 2020 | DDC 641.5/6362—dc23
        LC record available at https://lccn.loc.gov/2019057722

Trade Paperback ISBN: 978-1-9848-5717-0
eBook ISBN: 978-1-9848-5718-7

Printed in China

Art Direction and Design by Emma Campion
Food styling by Abby Stolfo
Prop styling by Claire Mack
Illustrations by Sarah Rose Weitzman

10 9 8 7 6 5 4 3 2 1

First Edition